SKIING IS A FAMILY SPORT!

SKIING
IS
A FAMILY SPORT!

JOHN HENRY AURAN

ASSOCIATION PRESS / NEW YORK

Copyright © 1970 by John Henry Auran

Association Press, 291 Broadway,
New York, N.Y. 10007

Second Printing - 1970

CONTENTS

ACKNOWLEDGEMENTS

Had it not been for some very skillful help and generous encouragement from a lot of nice people, it is doubtful if this book would ever have been produced. I owe special thanks to Hart and Harry Holmberg of the Hart Ski Co. for inspiring this project in the first place and to Doug Pfeiffer and *Skiing* Magazine for providing me with many of the technical photos that are used in this book. In addition, I would also like to express my thanks to photographers Virginia Sturgess, Piet Myers, Nancy Simmerman, Lloyd Hanson, Ray Thornton, Anne Simpkins, John Caldwell, Angela Hobin, and Ross Wagner; and Sun Valley, Aspen, Vail, Schweitzer Basin, Stowe, Steamboat, Waterville Valley, Incline Village, the French Tourist Office, and the Swiss Government Tourist Office for their help in providing me with suitable illustrations. Finally, I owe a special debt to my wife, Barbara, for her patience over the months that this book was being written and assembled.

J.H.A.

INTRODUCTION

It seems that everyone is skiing or wants to ski these days; it's an amazing phenomenon of our times. The daredevils ski, but that's to be expected. The phenomenon is the way whole families have become involved. Skiing has become the national family winter pastime.

It's amazing because skiing is a daring, exciting sport. But when you really think about it, it isn't so surprising that skiing has caught on rapidly as a family sport. Americans are an adventurous people, and what could be more adventurous than being outdoors in the winter, skiing down a mountain? And since skiing skill is within reach of everyone, young and old, why shouldn't it be a family sport?

You're probably thinking about the possibility of taking your family skiing right now, and I have a good idea of what is going through your mind: "I used to ski and loved it, but with kids and all, it's too complicated," or "We'd love to learn to ski, but with a family it's too expensive."

I'd be the last to claim that skiing is as simple as a stroll in the park or as economical as playing catch in the backyard. But as John Henry Auran, whom I can vouch for as one of the true authorities in skiing, so tellingly points out, both the complications and the expenses of skiing have been greatly exaggerated. And there are hundreds of thousands of skiing families to back up his words.

Although skiing used to be considered a sport only for the foolhardy, it was always a social sport. Even in the pioneering stages in the United States, when skiing for the most part meant ski jumping, the socializing was as important as the competition. If there was a jumper in the family—and in those days there were few Scandinavian families who didn't have at least one jumper—everybody down to fifth cousin used to turn out to see the family honor upheld. Between jumps, the clan gathered around the picnic baskets, which for the most part contained hot concoctions for keeping out the cold. A jumping meet was a social as well as a sporting occasion.

Skiing has changed tremendously since that pioneering era. Developments in teaching the sport, lifts and tows, equipment, and clothing have made skiing the sport of millions instead of a daredevil few. The members of the family are no longer spectators, but participants. Everyone is involved.

Despite the many changes which have made participation possible for the millions, skiing continues to share the socializing, the companionship, and the friendliness of the pioneering version of the sport. It's the one constant in the century in which skiing transformed itself from a necessity for snowbound Scandinavians into worldwide winter recreation.

No wonder it's a family sport!

I'm sure you will enjoy it.

HART HOLMBERG
President
Hart Ski Company

1

SKIING *IS* A FAMILY SPORT

What is skiing? Most simply put, skiing is a means of getting about in the snow with the help of two boards strapped to your feet. Of course, there is a great deal more to skiing and skis than that, as you'll see in the chapters that follow, but I want to emphasize the simple fundamentals because in skiing it is all too easy to get sidetracked by nonessentials—nonessentials which because of cost or time discourage people from taking part.

On the other hand, I don't want to mislead you. Some of the nonessentials are nevertheless useful, and in the minds of some not so nonessential. Most American skiers, for instance, would consider a lift to the top of the mountain a must. But just to show you it isn't necessarily so, consider the following experience.

An acquaintance of mine lives only a short distance from Mohawk Mountain, a small ski area in Connecticut. One weekend, he agreed to meet some friends at the area, and at the appointed hour he skied to the mountain on his touring skis. He found his friends in a long line waiting to get on the lift. Since they didn't want to give up their place in the line, he said he would meet them at the top of the hill for the run down. He then walked up the mountain by an easy route, and since they hadn't arrived, he skied down. His friends were still some distance from the lift loading point when he got to the bottom. He arranged a second rendezvous. This time he managed to arrive at the top a couple of minutes after his friends did. Aside from the fact that he was getting two runs for their every one, his expenditure for the day was 15 cents for a cup of hot chocolate. Theirs was $10 for two lift tickets and lunches.

Of course, this is an extreme example, but the point I want to make is that too many people look at skiing from too narrow a point of view. There is nothing wrong with taking lifts up the mountain, or with costly clothing and equipment, or long ski vacations at expensive and distant resorts, but these should be secondary to the prime objective of getting about in the snow, of being outdoors in the winter. Unfortunately, it is the more exotic aspects of skiing that get the most attention, and as a result of this somewhat one-sided reportage, a lot of families who could be on skis have decided that skiing is not for them.

Skiing is a family sport in which everyone can participate.

Despite these widely held misconceptions about skiing, the fog is beginning to lift. Every year more families are discovering that skiing is first-rate recreation, and because of that discovery, the ski population of the United States is doubling every five years. To use an overworked word, the sport is booming. And the major reason for the boom is the fact that skiing is gaining "recruits" not one at a time, but whole families at a time. Once one member of a family starts to ski, it is a safe bet that the others will quickly follow his example.

What's the big attraction?

Surprisingly, this isn't as easy a question to answer as you might think. Talk to a dozen skiers and you'll get at least a dozen answers. Some see skiing merely as a means of getting some outdoor exercise in winter. Others are fascinated by the challenge of speed and terrain. For some, it's a special snow condition, such as deep powder snow. For a few, it is the excitement of competition. For others still, it is the beauty of winter scenery. The reasons for going skiing seem endless.

Why then, if skiing is so subjective and individualistic a sport, does it have such a strong appeal to the family?

Well, a lot depends on what you mean by family sport. If you are thinking of family skiing as a sort of team game on snow, or as an exercise in tight-knit togetherness, skiing may not seem to qualify in your eyes. Except for the unusual situation where all members of the family are starting to learn to ski at the same time, or all have reached the same level of proficiency, a family will rarely ski together as a group all through the day. Usually the members of the family get together for a few runs before lunch or at the end of the day, but the way things usually go in skiing is that father, who probably had some skiing experience in college, will be on the expert slopes with his friends, mother and daughter will be on the intermediate trail practicing their christies, while the youngest will be in the children's play class at the bottom of the mountain.

What really makes skiing tick as a family sport is that every member, regardless of age, sex, or skill, can participate. Tod-

From the toddler on the left to former Olympic champion Roger Staub, every-one can find pleasure on skis.

dlers barely able to walk can be put on skis, and so can their grandparents. The longevity record in this respect probably belongs to Herman Smith-Johanssen, a durable, Norwegian-born Canadian who can still be seen gliding along the Maple Leaf Trail even though he is over 90 years old. And although he is, of course, an exception, skiers in their 60's and 70's are not. It is not at all unusual for three generations of a family to be skiing on the same mountain—and don't automatically assume that the older people will be found only on the easiest trail. Considering that the sport as we know it today is only a little more than 30 years old, it has caught on remarkably quickly as a family recreation.

Skiing has caught on as it has because it is really a very easy sport in which to get started. No matter how spastic you or a member of your family claims to be, it usually doesn't take long to learn the basic maneuvers that make it possible to get around on a mountain. But I should immediately add that as easy as it is to get started, as difficult it is to achieve perfection. Of course, that's part of skiing's fascination. No matter how much you learn about it, you will find that there are always new possibilities—in snow conditions, in trails and slopes, and mountains.

If the challenges of skiing are seemingly endless and seem to call for a lifetime of participation, the sport has the virtue of rewarding every level of skill. To be a duffer in golf or tennis, for instance, is usually a frustrating and often a humiliating experience. To be a more or less permanent denizen of the intermediate trails may not win any medals in skiing, but at least there isn't that ever-present score to remind you of your lowly status. Your young son may not be the last word in skiing elegance, but this doesn't deprive him of the satisfactions that the expert enjoys.

The absence of a score in skiing is a big attraction to many families. In too many family activities there is a tendency for the emphasis to be on the competitive element instead of on the activity itself, which all too frequently exacerbates existing sibling rivalries. As a result, many youngsters refuse to participate either because they know that their brother or sister can beat them, or because there's been some past misunderstanding about the rules of the game. In skiing, the only "opponent" is the mountain and the snow conditions. Of course, skiing has its competitive aspects too, but they are not essential in enjoying the sport. It is possible to have exciting skiing without being in a race, and there are skiers who have been at it for twenty years or more without ever having stepped into the starting gate. This is not to discourage competition among those who thrive on it, but merely to make the point that the satisfaction in skiing is in doing it—and without reference to either an opponent or an arbitrary mathematical standard.

This is why many youngsters who are unable to find a niche for themselves in the athletic programs offered by their schools frequently find satisfaction in skiing. And once they take it up, they are usually surprised to discover that they are not as unathletic as they thought. This invariably encourages parents to give skiing a try. Because their opportunities for outdoor recreation in winter are limited, they are only too happy to join in the fun.

That is why whole families are going skiing, and doing more of it every year. Skiing used to mean a long haul to the mountains, but because of increased participation it is now economically feasible to bring skiing close to the homes of millions of Americans for whom the sport used to be hundreds of miles away. Thanks to artificial snowmaking—an ingenious process that produces real skiing snow by mixing compressed air and water—almost any vicinity which has prolonged periods of below-freezing temperatures and anything resembling a hill can have skiing. If this isn't the case already where you live, it is bound to happen in the near future.

Convinced? Let's get down to particulars.

Sun Valley pays special attention to families and beginning skiers. Dollar Mountain is devoted exclusively to those who are new to skiing.

2

EQUIPMENT, CLOTHING, AND COMMON SENSE

Let's be realistic. Skiing is not the cheapest form of recreation. The fact that it is done in the winter makes clothing requirements much more critical than in summer activities. And the nature of the sport requires that every participant have his own equipment—either borrowed, rented, or bought.

Looking at clothing and equipment from the top end of the price scale, it is not at all difficult to spend $400, or more, for a complete outfit per person. An aspiring skier with a family will look at this figure—and quit right there. Which is too bad, because for that amount of money it is possible to do fairly well for a family of four if common sense is used. Let's look at some more reasonable ways to solve the clothing and equipment problems of the skiing family.

CLOTHING

Many skiing families who carefully watch their pennies do not usually consider ski clothing as a separate item in their clothing budget, unless, of course, they live in an area where the winter climate is mild. Ski wear is immensely versatile and can be used for all sorts of outdoor activity during fall and winter, particularly for children. For a few dollars extra you can get a first-rate ski wardrobe in lieu of the cold-weather outfits you usually buy. Prices for ski clothing range from the modest to the outrageous, but experience has shown that medium-priced items styled along classic lines give the best value for money spent. With a minimum of care, they will last many years, even with fairly heavy use.

It should be almost needless to say that the key function of ski clothing is to keep you warm and dry, but in any ski area, it is surprising how many people are improperly clothed. Not only do these people suffer needlessly from the cold, but they're so bulked up with heavy jackets, sweaters, and mufflers that they also have difficulty in executing the basic ski maneuvers.

At this point, two key rules concerning ski clothing should be emphasized:

1. Multiple layers of relatively light clothing are better than a single layer of heavy clothing. Multiple layers not only trap more body heat, but they make it possible to reduce the amount of clothing when you begin to overheat—and you will be surprised how often that happens, even during the coldest part of the ski season.

When you outfit the family, shop carefully and by all means get expert advice.

2. Ski clothes should fit snugly without being tight. Clothes that are too loose or too tight will cause loss of body heat.

An important corollary of these rules is to keep ski clothing dry and clean. Dirt and moisture conduct heat and quickly cancel the clothing's heat-trapping function. The major problem in this respect is excessive perspiration. Most beginning skiers, who have to work harder than experienced skiers, tend to overdress and find themselves sweating heavily under their many layers of clothing. Then they get cold when they rest. Their first reaction is to think that they are not dressed warmly enough when the very opposite is true.

Here is a rundown of clothing items that every skier should have:

Underwear: One set of long underwear is essential. It should not be too heavy. If the weather is very cold, it can be supplemented by so-called fishnet underwear, which is worn next to the skin. The fishnet underwear has large air pockets capable of trapping large amounts of body heat. Some skiers who prefer lighter outer clothing wear fishnet underwear all the time.

Turtlenecks: These shirts have snug closures around the neck and the wrists, and for this reason make excellent body-heat trappers. Some skiers dispense with the long underwear top and start with the turtleneck. Because it is snug-fitting and comes in a wide variety of colors and designs, it is useful for around-the-clock wear and gives variety to the skier's wardrobe. The only thing to guard against in buying turtlenecks is to make sure that the collars and wristbands are properly reinforced so that they don't stretch out after a few washings.

Sweaters: At least one sweater is necessary and there is a wide choice available in prices ranging from about $10 to $70. While almost any sweater will do for skiing, most ski sweaters are somewhat heavier than those you would buy normally for everyday use. Also, most skiers prefer a sweater with a somewhat harder, smoother finish because it doesn't pick up snow as readily as one that has a fuzzy finish.

Parkas: The parka is the main protective item against the snow, cold, wind, and wet. Although used for many other purposes than skiing, in its current form—lightweight, flexible, and stylish—it was first popularized by skiers who found its triple-layer construction consisting of a liner, insulating material, and wind- and water-resistant outer shell ideal for the sport. Available in prices ranging from $20 to $85, the cost of parkas is determined to a large extent by the insulating material. Of these materials good down is the most expensive, but it is also the lightest and warmest.

There are all kinds of parka designs, but the style preferred by most skiers is one that covers the fanny so that they have something warm to sit on when riding up on the chairlift. Most skiing parkas are also a bit roomier through the chest and across the shoulders so that there is room for a sweater underneath.

Windshirts: A windshirt made of tightly-woven nylon or silk is a useful if not essential item. These shirts are worn under the sweater and are ideal when the sun is out and the weather is too warm for a parka. You will find that the sun reflecting off the snow is quite warm when you're standing still, but when you are skiing at speed the wind will blow through your sweater and make you feel chilly. For those occasions, a windshirt, costing from $5 to $10, is a good solution.

Pants: Here you have three basic choices—stretch pants in various styles, warm-up pants, and knickers. Stretch pants range in price from $20 to $95; warm-up pants from $15 to $45; and knickers from $12 to $30. If the lower cost of knickers attracts you, keep in mind that they require a pair of heavy, kneelength socks which cost anywhere from $5 up. Most skiers opt for full length pants because open stockings have a tendency to pick up snow.

Although stretch pants have a great amount of give, care should be taken that they are fitted properly. There are a good many pitfalls in fitting stretch pants, especially the type whose cuff fits over the top of the boot. If you've had no experience with them, it's best to put yourself into the hands of a person who knows how. They should feel snug, but not tight. When the ankle straps are under the heel, you should feel some pull at the waist, but not so much that it feels uncomfortable. Also keep in mind that a pair of stretch pants is not a substitute for a girdle.

Children and some slim-hipped adults may get the feeling that they cannot keep the pants up. In that event, a pair of suspenders will alleviate the losing feeling.

One of the big attractions of stretch pants is that they wear well and will not bag at the knees as readily as most regular pants. However, the latter statement should not be taken to mean that they will not bag at all. When you sit down for any length of time, take the heel straps off so that the stretch material is not under constant strain. And at night, lay the pants flat instead of hanging them up. This allows the stretch material to recover from the strains of the day.

Warm-ups are a relatively new development. They were originally designed for racers to wear over regular ski pants and had full-length zippers down the sides so that they could be taken off easily. Since they have become popular with pleasure skiers—particularly younger skiers—not all of them have full zippers, but they can be worn with jeans and other tight pants. Warm-up pants are not as stylish as stretch pants, nor do they have quite the utility for off-slope wear. But they do come in a greater variety of colors and patterns, which makes them especially appealing to youngsters.

Socks: Most skiers wear two pairs of socks, one light pair next to the skin, and one pair of heavy wool or thermal socks on top of these.

Socks should be fitted carefully so that they are not so loose as to lump up when you pull on your boots, nor so tight as to restrict circulation. If you find that your feet are still cold, you might try the following trick;

Keep the socks warm and do not put them on until you are ready to go out skiing. The trouble with ski socks is that they are too warm for most people when they are worn indoors. As a result the socks get damp, and damp socks are almost impossible to warm up once they are chilled.

Hats: A hat is more important than you may think. It not

only keeps ears warm, but also plays a role in keeping the rest of your body comfortable. A vast amount of blood is pumped through your head, and if it is exposed, the loss of body heat is considerable.

Gloves and mittens: Most skiers will prefer gloves rather than mittens because of the finger freedom they allow for holding poles and fastening bindings. Mittens, however, are much warmer.

In either event, ski gloves or mittens should be made of leather with some sort of insulating lining. The leather helps keep off the wind and also protects the hands in case of a fall. On extra cold days use a wool liner for added warmth.

Ski gloves and mittens should be somewhat roomier than ordinary gloves and they should also have a cuff long enough to cover the wrist.

EQUIPMENT

The cost of clothing is easy enough to justify. Ski equipment is useful only for skiing. How can the initial "bite" be reduced to a minimum, at least until you and your family know for sure you really like the sport?

Most people get started in skiing when a friend urges them to come along. He may have suitable equipment that you can borrow, but in that case be sure that it is really suitable. Nothing will kill interest in skiing faster than oversized boots or skis too long or too stiff for easy learning. But assuming that the equipment you can borrow fits your family's needs—use the section following to determine if it does—don't stop there. Take boots, poles, and skis to a ski shop and have them checked over for any minor repairs or adjustments that may be necessary. If these have to be done after you get to the ski area, they are irritating, time-consuming, and invariably more expensive than if you had done the job in the city before you left.

If you can't borrow equipment, it can be rented by the day or for a longer period of time, either at ski areas or in cities. Renting from a reputable shop makes it much more likely that you will get what you need. Most shops that rent have a wide choice, particularly in boots, which are the most critical item in the skier's outfit. Complete outfits rent anywhere from $3.50 to $10 a day, depending on the quality of equipment rented. Most shops will deduct the rental fee, or at least part of it, if you subsequently decide to buy your skis, poles and boots.

There are some shops which rent or lease ski outfits by the season. Season-long fees run from 60 to 70 per cent of the cost of a new outfit, less of course when the outfit has already seen some use.

Incidentally, beginning skiers aren't the only ones who rent. People who ski only once or twice a season find it more economical to do so, as do skiers who live in snowless regions and whose only skiing is done during an annual ski vacation.

Even if a novice skier finds he's hooked on the sport, it might be wise for him to delay buying until he has learned to

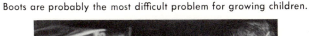

Boots are probably the most difficult problem for growing children.

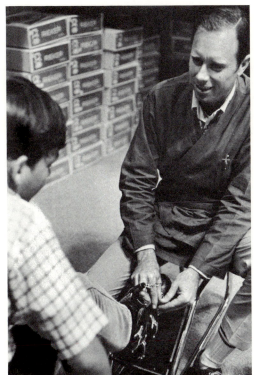

make stem christies. Skis that are ideal for the beginner have their limitations in faster skiing. Novice skiers, particularly the more athletic, will save themselves some money if they don't have to switch after passing through the beginning stages. Incidentally, the amount of time it takes to pass through these stages depends on a variety of factors, which are discussed in the next chapter.

Most skiers who rent equipment are ready to buy long before their budget is ready to stand the strain. Rather than dreaming up schemes to get the money together, renting provides a simple, common-sense way to enjoy the benefits of your own personal equipment without the financial sweat.

Boots: Even if you have no particular budget limitations, the first item on the equipment agenda is boots, and there are very good reasons why this is so.

Boots represent the vital link between you and your skis. If they are too big or too soft, they make control of the skis extremely difficult, if not impossible. If they are too tight or have pressure spots, your feet will not only get cold, but your whole skiing experience will be miserable as well.

It is important not to judge ski boots by hiking boot standards. The boot should feel snug, and it will feel relatively heavy. And because it is designed to transmit the slightest motion of your feet to the skis, it will feel stiff.

A good boot should be almost unyielding laterally—that is, it should keep you from rolling your ankle from side to side. However, it should allow for some forward–backward ankle movement, but not so much that you cannot put pressure on the tips of your skis. It should also have a sole rigid enough that the boot will not twist when you are turning or traversing on a slope. It should be durable—skiing puts tremendous stress on boots—and, of course, it should keep your feet warm.

To fulfill all these functions, a ski boot requires the ultimate in the boot-making art. Not surprisingly then, boots are relatively expensive, and even a second-rate pair will cost more than a very good pair of shoes. If you examine a boot carefully and compare the amount of material in your shoes with that in

Some choices in boots: *Lower left,* competition-type boot with a high shaft is most suitable for the expert skier. *Lower right,* heavy-duty buckle boot for advanced men and women skiers. *Center,* child's three-buckle boot, a really useful item for youngsters who still haven't the strength to lace up their boots. *Top left,* plastic laminated boot which comes in several colors for better women skiers. *Top right,* typical buckle boot in the medium-priced range for men.

the boot you will readily see why. Add to that the complexity of the ski boot structure and the special machinery required to manufacture it, and the reason for the price becomes clear, if not any easier to take.

If you want a boot that will last you several years—between five and seven—plan to spend about $70, give or take $10. What you'll actually buy will depend more on fit and features, and these can throw off your calculation in either direction.

While you may have your mind set on a particular type of boot, don't insist on it at all costs. The key to the boot-fitting problem is the last on which the manufacturer builds his boot. These lasts vary from manufacturer to manufacturer, and the boot you have your eye on may be built on a last that does not fit your feet. So be prepared to go to another brand, even if this involves a few dollars more. Remember, fit is everything.

There are several types of boots which you may want to consider. Basically, there are boots which are laced up or buckled up; boots made of leather, plasticized leather, and plastic; and boots fitted by the standard sizes or customized to your foot by means of various plastic foams. As this is being written, there is a virtual revolution in ski boots and changes are coming fast. Today's latest feature is commonplace tomorrow. It's something to keep in mind if you happen to yearn for the latest wrinkle. If it is out of reach this season, it could well be available in a lower price range next year.

At the bottom of the price scale are lace boots of leather. For between $25 and $50, they can provide satisfactory performance for a couple of seasons for children and casual skiers. If you are buying in this range, try to step up at least to a double boot—it has a soft inner boot for both added comfort and extra support—since single lace boots are usually very little more than a means of holding your skis to your feet.

The lacing is something of a nuisance. If you lace too tight or too loose or have a wrinkle in your sock, you have to start the process all over again, and if you're not used to lacing ski boots, it's a hard process. That's the reason why most of the boots now sold have some sort of buckle system. The number of buckles can vary from one to six, but this is not a particularly crucial consideration since the number depends on the design of the boot. However, most better adult ski boots have five buckles.

The advantage of buckles is not only that the boots are easier to put on, but that adjustments for fit and comfort can be made throughout the day. As the day goes on, the feet have a tendency to shrink slightly. With buckles, in contrast with laces, it is no chore to take up the slack. In fact, many skiers unbuckle after every run and buckle up again after they get to the top of the hill. The cost of this convenience is from $5 to $10 above that of comparable lace boots when available.

(Lace boots are no longer being made in the medium and upper price brackets.)

Because boots are such a critical factor in getting good response out of skis, and because they have to take tremendous stresses and abuse, leather boots break down rather quickly. They stretch and get soft and are no longer able to transmit the subtle motions that are needed to ski, particularly under difficult conditions. Until a few years ago, the answer was to go to stiffer and stiffer boots as your skiing improved and as you did more of it. This was not only expensive, but the boots also took almost heroic measures to break in. That's when plastic came into the picture.

It would take a book to describe all the ways in which plastic is used in ski boots, but the boots themselves break down into two basic types: those using plasticized leather and those made completely of plastic. Both types are capable of giving the very best of performance although the somewhat more expensive all-plastic boots seem to have captured the fancy of the best skiers, probably because they are virtually immune to stretching and can be manipulated more readily for a closer fit. On the other hand, skiers with sensitive feet still prefer boots made with leather (even if it is plasticized) on the grounds that leather breathes and is more comfortable to wear.

The fact that a boot is made of plasticized leather or plastic is in itself no guarantee of high quality. Boots of plasticized leather are available from $50 and up, in all-plastic from about $80 and up. Fortunately, the boot business is so competitive that price is a good indication of quality, at least in a first-rate ski shop, so the further your budget will stretch, the better the boot you will get.

The ultimate refinement in ski boots is custom fitting with the use of plastic foams of various types. This involves fitting the boot in the shop and is a time-consuming and expensive proposition—about $100 a pair and up. It would not be worth mentioning in connection with family skiing except that the concept looks promising and may be available at less than stratospheric prices in the next few years. In that case, the "foamed boots," as they are called, may be a good solution for children's boots, which is the major equipment headache for skiing families. A youngster who would normally need replacement boots every year or two could have one top-quality outer shell for several years and be refoamed as needed. But that is still very much in the future.

Regardless of price or concept, fitting ski boots is no easy matter. Your best bet is to go to a specialty ski shop with a reputation for a good fit. Unless you yourself are familiar with what a good fit feels like, only a specialist can tell whether a boot is right. Furthermore, he has special equipment and skills to modify the boots for accuracy of fit and to remove pressure points if any exist.

If the boot fits correctly, break-in should not be too much of a problem. Most skiers can break in boots by wearing them around the house before they actually use them for skiing. However, don't be surprised if you have to take the boots back for a few adjustments after your first outing. Fit is rarely perfect the first time around.

Finally, the life of your boots depends on the care that you give them. If they are leather, polish them with the special ski boot polish the manufacturer recommends—in many cases, ordinary shoe polish won't do—and if they have leather soles, treat them from time to time with a sealing compound. Both products are available from your ski shop. Even plastic boots need a certain amount of care. Be alert to buckle problems and small cracks or cuts. As long as they are minor, they can still be fixed. If you let them go, breaks can enlarge rapidly and damage the boots beyond repair.

Bindings: After you have bought your boots, the next major purchase you make should be bindings. Theoretically, it doesn't make sense to own a pair of bindings without a pair of skis, but the reasoning here is that a second-rate pair of skis can do less damage than a second-rate pair of bindings. Furthermore, a good pair of bindings will outlast every other item of ski equipment. The good release bindings, first introduced about 10 years ago, are still giving good service today. Barring a major breakthrough in binding technology, the good pair you buy today is capable of giving you a lifetime of service, providing, of course, there is reasonable care and maintenance.

Bindings come in a variety of designs. Select one made by a reliable manufacturer.

There are two basic types of bindings on the market—nonreleasable bindings and releasable bindings. A nonreleasable binding, commonly called a "bear trap" by skiers, is basically nothing more than a stiff piece of metal shaped like a shallow, squared-up U and tapered in such a way that it can hold the toe of the boot. To hold the boot in the "bear trap," there is some sort of cable arrangement with a clamp. The reason for all this description is that if someone tries to get you to use skis with such bindings you can recognize them and quickly and firmly decline the offer.

A releasable binding consists of some sort of pivoting toe unit—there are several types, which work on several different principles—and either a cable whose release mechanism is built into the latching lever or a special heel release unit. The function of the toe unit is to protect your legs in the event of a twisting fall. The function of the release at the heel is to protect you from the consequences of an overhead fall.

If you are the downhill-only type, a heel release unit is a far safer bet. However, if you plan to do a little touring the edge should go to cable releases. Climbing for any length of

Binding installation designed for children is easy to operate.

time with skis on requires that the heel be free to move up and down, at least a little bit. This is only possible with a cable release and a special touring adapter (more on this later).

Regardless of the releasable binding combination you finally pick, it is vital that you fully understand how the binding functions and how it is adjusted. A good ski shop will do its best to adjust your bindings correctly when they are first mounted on the skis, but for a variety of reasons bindings can easily get out of whack and you should learn to adjust them yourself.

In selecting bindings, there is a large choice of brands in a relatively narrow price range. Although price isn't everything, approach any combination under $25 with caution unless it is specifically designed for children. Be prepared to go as high as $45. It is a good idea to stick to established brands. And if you select a toe unit of one brand, it is best that you buy a heel release by the same manufacturer unless you and your shop are absolutely certain that a brand mixture will work.

For more information on binding adjustment and other aspects of safety see Chapter 6.

Skis: Buying boots and bindings is a fairly straightforward proposition. The real excitement is in picking a pair of skis. The selection seems almost limitless, and, as one skier said, "It's almost like picking the girl you're going to marry. You don't really know what you have until you've married her."

You will find it easier to keep your perspective if you keep certain fundamentals in mind. Wood skis range in price from the tot's simple models starting at $10 to about $80. Metal and fiberglass skis run anywhere from $80 to over $250. If you are a purely recreational skier, ignore anything over $60 in wood skis, and any model over $165 in metal or fiberglass skis. Skis above these prices are usually either specialized models for the racer or super-expert or they have features of benefit only to those who do a great deal of skiing.

Although wood skis cost considerably less initially, they have the drawback of having a severely limited useful skiing life. Even with the best of care, wood skis begin to lose their skiing characteristics after a couple of seasons and, after that time, their trade-in value is virtually zero.

Fiberglass (or plastic, or epoxy) skis are valued, particularly by better skiers, because they come closest to the best qualities of both fine wood and metal skis and in most respects surpass them. There are many different designs on the market, and because they are relatively new on the skiing scene, many of these designs are still in a state of development. Because of this, there are serious questions about the skis' durability and repairability. If you have your heart set on a pair of fiberglass skis, it is best to take a critical look at the warranty before buying.

Probably the best bet for the recreational skier are metal skis. As a general rule, they are not only the easiest to ski on, but they are reasonably unbreakable and usually carry the best warranties. Metal skis need very little maintenance during and between seasons and they can be reconditioned after several years of service at nominal cost. Experts will argue about the capabilities of metal skis on ice and at very high speeds, but these arguments amount to little more than nitpicking as far as the average skier is concerned.

Having decided whether it will be wood, fiberglass, or metal, the next question to settle is the model you will need. Although a given brand of skis may have different names for its models, basically they break down as follows: *Standard,* for novices,

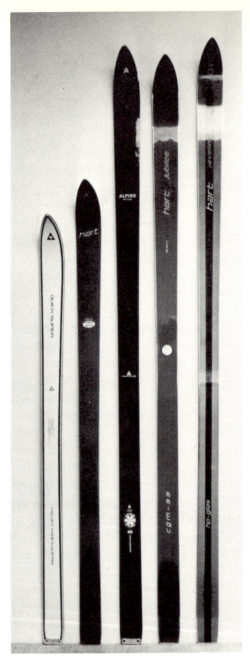

Skis come in many brands and models. *Left,* a medium-priced wood ski suitable for children up to about the teens. *Second from left,* for the ambitious young-ster, a metal ski which is also suitable for racing. *Center,* a typical wood ski for the adult beginner. *Second from right,* a recreational metal ski for novices and intermediates. *Right,* a top performer for advanced and expert skiers made of metal and fiberglass.

most intermediates, and casual skiers; *Combination,* for good
intermediates and advanced skiers, and for fairly serious recreational skiers; and *Competition,* which are made with special
dimensions and characteristics to make them suitable for each
of the Alpine racing events—downhill, slalom, and giant slalom. Although the label Competition may be quite imposing,
don't totally overlook the potential of these racing models. In
the first place, the label is used quite loosely, more or less to
indicate the basic characteristics of the skis; and, second, competition skis can be used to solve special problems of strong,
athletic skiers, and of skiers who ski a great deal under special
conditions, such as ice. For a more detailed discussion of
what's involved in each of these racing events see Chapter 9 on
competition.

In addition to these basic models, you should be familiar
with two special-purpose models: *deep powder* and *short* skis.
Deep powder skis are especially flexible so that they don't dive
in very deep or very soft snow. They are not very satisfactory
on packed snow, and unless you live in a region where there
is lots of deep, light powder, it is best to rent them when your
family is faced with these conditions. Short skis are something
else again, and a matter of great controversy among skiers and
instructors. For purposes of definition, a short ski is one that is
shorter than you are tall. In addition, there are so-called short-
shorts, ranging anywhere from 30 inches up to 5 feet in length.
These short skis are not scaled-down adult models, but have
special dimensions to make them more suitable for use by
average-sized and larger adults. Whether you should buy a
pair is something you will have to decide for yourself. Most
skiers find that short skis lack stability once they graduate to
faster skiing. The big advantage of short skis is that they are
easy to turn. Because of this, they deserve consideration by the
"just once in a while" skier.

You are now in the ball park, but you're not quite through
yet. Although such designations as Standard and Combination
represent general standards, each manufacturer has his own
interpretation of these general standards and may, in fact, have

several models in each general category. These models may have differences in skiing characteristics, but just as frequently the differences may be in the way of features. Your ski shop should be able to advise you on these points.

How do you know whether you will like the skis you have selected?

Providing you give him the right information, a good ski salesman should be able to size you and your family up and provide you with skis that will make you happy. But if you are skeptical, you have a couple of alternatives. You can ask a friend or acquaintance who may have a similar model what his experience has been with the ski. Or you can rent or borrow a pair of skis of the same model for a tryout. Most ski shops have at least one pair of each model they stock mounted with bindings for just such tryouts. If these tryout pairs are your size, well and good. If not, you may have to prevail on your friends.

If you cannot try out the skis and cannot get expert advice, here are a few rules of thumb that may help you:

- If you are a novice or casual skier choose a ski three to six inches above your head; if you are a fairly proficient skier (you should be able to do a stem christie), the skis should be six to 12 inches above your head; if you are an advanced or expert skier from nine to 15 inches above your head.

- Skis should have between three-fourths of an inch and an inch-and-a-half of camber (arch) when they are put bottom to bottom at the tips and tails.

- A more flexible ski is easier to use than one that is stiffer. Flex is a fairly complex characteristic to determine because the flex can vary at various points along the ski. However, overall, a soft flex is one that enables you to squeeze the skis together between thumb and forefinger.

- If you are tall for your weight, choose a ski with a somewhat softer flex. If you are husky, choose a somewhat stiffer ski.

- If your skiing is done primarily on hardpacked slopes in the East and Midwest, a stiffer ski is in order than if most of your skiing is done in softer snow in the West.

- Women usually take a softer ski than men of the same height.
- If you don't know how much to spend for skis, but have an over-all budget, figure to spend about 40 per cent on skis.
- Skis should be perfectly flat and true across the bottoms. Flatness can be determined with a straight edge placed across the bottom. Trueness can be established by putting the skis bottom to bottom at the tip and tail and determining that they touch at all corners. The second step involves sighting down the bottom of the ski to make sure that the tail of the ski is on the same plane as the tip.

In addition to these general points, examine the skis critically for good edges and good bottom finish. This is particularly important when buying lower-cost skis.

Good steel edges along the bottom of the skis are absolutely essential for control in Alpine skiing. They are either screwed on the ski in segments or bonded or welded to the ski as an integral part of the structure. Most of the better metal and plastic skis use one-piece edges, although it is not necessarily a sign of an inferior product if the edges happen to be segmented. The important consideration is that the edges be perfectly flush with the running surface and feel smooth to the touch both along the bottom and on the sides. Although the edges on good skis are made of hard steel, they will have to be sharpened periodically with a file or a special edge sharpener, particularly on days when there is lots of ice on the slopes.

All skis, even the cheapest, have some sort of special running surface. At the bottom end of the price scale, this surface is usually a painted-on lacquer, and it will require a coat of wax before it will slide easily. From that point up, manufacturers can use a variety of plastics, but with few exceptions, most of them use polyethylene of various densities. Polyethylene slides easily on most kinds of snow, and many skiers do not bother to wax it at all except on wet, warm snow. However, this is not a good practice. A thin coat of wax not only prevents the polyethylene from oxidizing, but also protects the bottom against minor scratches and bruises. A waxed ski also turns more easily and tracks better.

Polyethylene has the drawback of gouging and scratching relatively easily. The heavier, denser (and more expensive) polys reduce this hazard considerably but don't totally eliminate it. Fortunately, polyethylenes are easy to repair with a so-called candle and a soldering iron. The poly around the damaged spot is softened with the iron and filled with the drippings of the candle. After filing the patch flush and smoothing it with soft steel wool, the running surface is as good as new.

A final thought: Even though you have selected with care and on the best of recommendations, your new skis may give you quite a bit of trouble on your first few runs, particularly if you've switched to a more advanced model, or if you have changed from wood to metal or plastic. Don't immediately blame yourself for having made a bad buy. It takes a couple of days to really adapt to a new ski. Of course, if the trouble persists, have the skis checked by a ski shop, but the chances are that what you really need is a lesson to eliminate a bad habit you were getting away with on your old skis.

Poles: Poles play a larger role in skiing than most initiates think. They are more than just supports to keep you upright or levers to help you get up. You literally can't do without them if you expect to ski in the bumps and on steeper terrain.

To do their job, poles should be strong, light, and feel comfortable in the hand. Not surprisingly, a good pole has been compared with a good fencing sword.

The best poles are made of the highest grade aircraft aluminum alloy. These cost $20 and up, although you can get poles almost as good from $15. Below that point, the quality of material drops markedly, and it is doubtful whether you'll be ahead in the long run. Poles are vulnerable to bending and breaking. Since pole requirements are the same for every level of skill, it makes sense to spend the extra three or four dollars to get a good pair.

The "proper" pole length seems to change almost from year to year, but these changes are not really terribly significant.

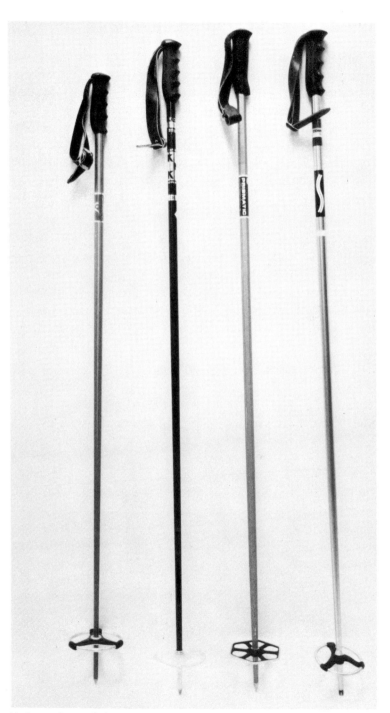

Modern poles are light, strong, and colorful. Here's a selection ranging in price from $10 to $35.

Whatever the fashion may be, you won't be far off if you select a pair of poles whose grip passes comfortably under your armpits when the point is on the floor next to your heel. Don't lift your shoulder when passing the poles under your arm.

Poles require little in the way of maintenance. Check the basket from time to time to make sure that it doesn't pull off easily, and it's a good idea to check the screw that holds the grip and strap.

WHAT ELSE?

Skiing has numerous accessories, some essential, some merely helpful. The ones listed here will contribute greatly to your safety and skiing enjoyment.

Boot tree-carrier: If your boot soles are made of leather, a boot tree with a clamping action is essential to keep the soles from curling. Curled boots can keep releasable bindings from

Boot press or carrier prevents boot sole curl, a major cause of binding malfunction.

releasing. If you have sealed or molded boot soles, the tree is not so essential, but is still a great convenience for carrying your boots.

Arlberg straps: These straps, fastened to the cables or to the heel unit (if you use step-ins) are an absolute must. They keep the skis from running wildly down the hill in the event the binding releases. They not only save you a humiliating walk to the bottom, but they also keep the ski from impaling innocent bystanders.

Goggles: There are weather conditions when goggles are absolutely essential, particularly on cold days when your eyes will water readily. Use the yellow lenses when the day is overcast and the light is flat. Use the green lenses when the sun is out. Never ski without some sort of dark glasses on sunny days. The glare off the snow is intense and gets progressively stronger as the altitude gets higher. To keep the goggles from fogging, they should be put on inside and kept on at all times. If this doesn't work, enlarge the vent holes or slits with a knife or razor blade. Some anti-fog compounds may also work.

Ski rack: If you use a car for going skiing, a roof or trunk rack is necessary. Carrying skis inside the car (unless it happens to be a roomy station wagon) kills space and is hard on the upholstery. It is also dangerous in the event of a sudden stop or an accident. Of the two types of racks, a roof rack is more desirable since it doesn't block access to the trunk or the engine (if it's a rear-engined car).

Edge sharpener: Edge sharpening is a job that can be done by your ski shop, but if you follow instructions that come with several edge sharpeners on the market you can do the job yourself. Having one handy can save a day of skiing if you run into unexpected icy conditions.

Ski ties: Many skiers disdain the use of ski ties when carrying their skis, preferring to use their Arlberg straps to hold them together. However, using the straps isn't enough to keep the skis from sliding against each other and in the process dulling the edges. Ski ties do the job, and for only a few cents.

Wax kit: As already mentioned a coat of wax is good for

your ski bottoms. A small wax kit with three or four waxes costs about a dollar. It isn't necessary to carry it on you during the colder months, but you should have it handy from mid-March on or whenever you suspect you will run into variable conditions.

Belt bag or small rucksack: All the odds and ends a skier is apt to carry are difficult to stow away in pants and parka pockets. The problem is compounded when you're carrying supplies for the whole family. A leather belt bag is ideal for lots of small accessories, a rucksack is better if you want to carry food and extra clothing.

In this chapter I have dealt only with Alpine equipment and generally with adults in mind. Because touring equipment is so simple, it is treated separately as part of Chapter 8. As far as Alpine equipment for children is concerned, the same standards as for adult equipment apply. However, equipment for children poses some special problems. These are covered in detail in Chapter 5.

The advantages of attending ski school are many. Not only do you learn faster, but you are safer, particularly in the beginner stages.

3

LEARN TO SKI...THE EASY WAY

How long does it take to learn to ski? Should my family take lessons? Are they expensive? Can we teach ourselves? These are some of the frequently asked questions I have encountered in my ten years as a ski writer. I usually try to evade these questions, not because they cannot be answered, but because to me they indicate a piecemeal approach to learning to ski. I like to look at the problem in a somewhat different way.

There is a better way of going about this business of learning to ski—and that way takes you and your family through ski school. Not only will ski school assure that all of you will learn the various maneuvers in their proper sequence on terrain suitable for your levels of proficiency, but you will be in the company of others with the same problems that you have. In such company it becomes a lot easier to laugh at yourself.

If I have convinced you that ski school is the only proper medium for learning to ski, you are now prepared for a number of shortcuts which will reduce ski school time to a minimum.

Shortcut 1: Be in good physical condition. If yours is a physically active family, there's nothing special you have to do. Those a little soft around the middle will have to find a way to get themselves in shape (see Chapter 6 for suggestions). Recreational skiing makes no vast demands on physical strength, but it does require muscle and tendon flexibility. If your muscles are flexible, you reduce your chances of getting hurt, but equally important, it speeds up learning tremendously.

Shortcut 2: Rather than charging out and buying a full set of equipment right off the bat, rent shorter skis—no longer than you are tall. Shorter skis, while lacking in stability at higher speeds, reduce the time it takes to achieve mobility on skis. While you are learning, you won't miss the extra stability and you will find it a lot easier to maneuver your skis through the beginning lessons and exercises.

Shortcut 3: Make sure the members of your family are familiar with their equipment before they get on the ski slope. Using this book as a guide, see to it they know how to get into and out of their bindings. You can make a family game out of putting on and taking off skis on your living-room floor until all of you are thoroughly familiar with the procedure. Do the

Learn how to hold your pole properly. The strap must rest on the back of your hand before you grasp the grip. If the strap doesn't support the heel of your hand when you're holding the pole, adjust the strap or have it shortened.

same with the poles. And have them learn to get a snug lace or buckle job without cutting off circulation. Familiarity with the equipment can save a tremendous amount of time that's taken out of lessons because skis can't be put back on without help or because of the agony of incorrectly laced up boots.

Shortcut 4: Get the feel of your skis before taking a lesson. If yours is a good, pebble-free lawn and you don't mind getting stared at by the neighbors (kids don't mind), go out and slide around on your skis (with a coat of wax for protection). Walk around, sit down and get up, do step turns and kick turns, and

Getting up from a fall. Pull yourself together, bring the skis straight across the slope and well under you. Usually it is quite easy to stand up at this point, but if you have trouble take support from your poles.

all the other so-called static maneuvers of skiing. Of course, if there is snow on the ground, so much the better. But don't try anything that's too complicated. Don't develop bad habits before you get started. Getting the feel of your skis is a good idea any time before you start to ski or before taking a lesson.

Shortcut 5: Learn skiing terminology. Ski instructors will try to keep beginning lessons as uncomplicated as possible, but sometimes there's no way around a technical term. Knowing what it means can save time taken out for explanations. It also makes skiing more fun when you talk with other skiers.

Shortcut 6: Try to get as much continuity into your family's lessons as possible. From a safety point of view, it makes all the sense in the world to have them stay in ski school until they are capable of at least a competent stem christie and, preferably, a fairly sound parallel turn. This may not be possible for reasons of time or money. But once you've made up your mind they should learn, try to have them stay with lessons for a fairly concentrated period of time. Especially in the beginning stages, space lessons no further than a week or two apart. If you don't think you can swing this financially, it is better to wait a little while until you can assure this continuity.

A single lesson costs about $4, and variations from this rate are not significant enough to worry about. You can reduce the cost of lessons at many ski areas by buying a ticket for both the morning and afternoon session—each session is about two hours long—or by buying a block of tickets for a group of ten lessons, usually for between $30 and $35. By buying a group of lessons at one time, you more or less force yourself to make use of your investment.

If it is at all possible for you to find the time, a learn-to-ski week at a ski area is by far the best bet for you and your family from both a learning and a financial point of view. Learn-to-ski

Walking on skis is a fundamental. Practice on the flat, taking small steps at first. Keeping the upper body forward, set one foot solidly and plant the pole at the angle shown. Then *slide* the other leg forward. Try to get as much glide as possible between strides.

weeks are usually held during slower parts of the season—
before Christmas, during January, and from the last week of
March on—and there are sizable discounts available for both
lifts and lessons. For instance, at Mt. Snow in Vermont it is
possible to get a Monday through Friday package of five lessons and lifts for five days for as low as $27.50 per person. Of
course, on top of that there are the costs of lodging and meals,
but these are also substantially reduced during learn-to-ski
weeks. But more important than the economy are the benefits
of continuity in daily instruction.

Ski schools are organized along ability levels. There is at
least one instructor for each major ability level—beginner,
intermediate and advanced. Larger schools break these levels
down even finer, usually by the various maneuvers, such as
snow plow, stem turn, stem christie, etc.

After you've bought your lesson ticket, go to the ski school
assembly area, quite often marked by a big school bell. There
the director of the ski school will ask you what you can do. In
answering, be as precise as you possibly can. For instance, "I
just started on stem turns."

A lesson usually involves an explanation of the maneuver to
be practiced, a demonstration, and then execution by the students. After that come the corrections by the instructor; then
more of the same, but usually with variations. Not all instructors follow this procedure, so don't be disconcerted when your
instructor doesn't. Particularly in the more advanced classes,
there will be more skiing and less demonstration and explanation. You may not realize it, but what your instructor is doing
is guiding you over carefully selected terrain where the maneuvers you are doing come almost naturally. This also helps to
build your confidence, a big factor in skiing success.

For the most part your family will be taking group lessons
—that is, lessons with anywhere from 6 to 10 other students.
This arrangement is satisfactory most of the time. However,
occasionally you may find that you have a special problem that
seems to defy the usual remedies. In that case you should consider a private lesson where the instructor can concentrate on

your difficulty exclusively. Private lessons are relatively expensive—usually around $10 an hour—but worth it if your progress has come to a standstill.

There are two basic references to your position on the hill. You are either in the *fall line,* the shortest, most direct and steepest route down the slope, or you're on a *traverse,* which is any route at an angle to the fall line or, to put it another way, any route across the hill.

To refer to left and right can be confusing when you are describing skiing maneuvers since most of the body motions are in a direction opposite to the one you want to go. When you are on a traverse, everything on the side pointing to the top of the mountain is called *uphill,* everything on the side facing the bottom of the mountain is called *downhill.* This can be a little confusing when you traverse in the opposite direction when everything that was downhill becomes uphill and everything uphill becomes downhill.

While you are turning, the uphill-downhill designations are no longer adequate. From the moment you start to turn, instructors speak of the *inside,* meaning the side toward the center of the turn, and the *outside,* meaning the side to the outside of the turn. This is simple enough, except for the fact that inside and outside is also used to describe the edges of your skis, but not in the same frame of reference. As one popular instructor puts it, "The *inside edges* are on the big toe side of your foot and the *outside edges* are always on the little toe side of your foot . . . always."

When you think about it while reading this book these terms seem straightforward enough. But when you get on a slope whizzing along at what seems to you to be 100 miles an hour, it is hard to keep these directions in mind. If, as you get the feel of your equipment in your back-yard exercises, you sound out uphill, downhill, inside, outside, these skiing terms will be firmly fixed in your mind.

The next set of words are somewhat more complex and refer to a series of technical concepts common to every approach to skiing. There is more than one way of learning to ski and these ways are called *techniques, systems,* or *methods.* Hence the American technique, which is the way American ski schools teach everything from walking to wedeln. Do not confuse technique, system, or method with *exercises.* In a technique there is one prescribed way to execute a given maneuver, but there may be dozens of exercises to achieve the prescribed way. Unfortunately, a new exercise is frequently hailed as a new technique.

Probably the most important single concept in skiing is *edging* or *edge control.* It is through the use of the edges that you determine the bite of the ski on the snow. Any time your skis are not flat on the snow, they are edged. The more they are edged, the sharper the bite. The amount of bite is controlled primarily by knees and ankles and this usually requires some sort of compensating movement of your body. This compensatory movement is called *angulation.* Assume for a moment that you are sliding across the hill in a traverse. To keep yourself from slipping off the hill, you push your knees into the hill to increase the amount of edging. If you push only the knees into the hill, the position would be extremely unstable since your weight would no longer be directly over the skis. To correct this situation, you lean the body back over the skis, in other words you *angulate.* Some instructors describe angulation as pinching at the waist.

In recreational skiing, most of the skier's weight is carried on the downhill ski. Therefore, in order to turn and still retain control of the skis, there must be a *weight shift* from the downhill ski to the downhill-ski-to-be; or, to put it another way, from the downhill ski in the traverse to the outside ski of the intended turn. In the elementary maneuvers, weight shift is a pronounced stepping from ski to ski. As the skier progresses, the weight shift becomes more subtle.

All turns in which the skis are parallel during the end phases of the turn are called *christies.* In order to make a christie, the skis must ride on the edges toward the inside of the turn. In all but one skiing situation this requires an edge change. This can be done one edge at a time, or simultaneously. In *stemmed* turns, the outside-ski-to-be is angled slightly to point in the direction of the intended turn. In the process of angling the ski, it is put on its inside edge. Weight is then shifted onto this ski and the other ski is brought alongside, its edge also being changed in the process.

In parallel skiing there are two additional concepts: *unweighting* and *turning force*. In parallel skiing both skis have to start the turn simultaneously. Therefore, angling the skis and changing edges is out. To turn skis parallel the skis have to be *unweighted*. While the skis are unweighted, or light, the edges are changed and turning force is applied. This is done in one continuous motion.

The skis can be unweighted in two basic ways—by *up-unweighting* or by *down-unweighting*. Up-unweighting is done by rising sharply from the slight crouch which is the skier's basic stance. Down-unweighting is done by dropping the body sharply by collapsing the knees. The skis can also be made light by jumping them completely off the ground, or by skiing on to the crest of a small bump.

The turning force you apply to your skis can be a simple swiveling of the feet. For additional power you can call on either *rotation*—that is, turning your body in the direction of the turn—or *counter-rotation,* which requires that you turn your body in a direction opposite to that of the intended turn. Why both work well would require a long, technical explanation, which is outside the province of this book. However, you should be aware that both methods exist. As far as the United States and Canada are concerned, all but a few ski schools use the counter-rotational approach to ski instruction.

Because I feel strongly that novice and intermediate skiers belong in ski school, no attempt is made here to give you a full explanation of the various skiing maneuvers. The picture section is primarily intended to familiarize aspiring skiers with the various turns and to illustrate the major concepts that apply to them. There is no way for any book to come to grips with the thousands of problems skiers have. Only the individual attention of a skilled ski instructor can take care of those.

Sidestepping is not only a way to get up the hill, but an important exercise in gaining an understanding of edge control. In sidestepping you are going up the hill sideways, as the term implies. The first move is to transfer your weight to the lower ski, so that the upper one is free to move, and to prevent it from slipping you put it slightly on edge. You next move the upper ski uphill, lightly slamming it into the snow to get a firm purchase. Then transfer your weight to the upper ski, pulling the lower ski uphill. This maneuver, over long distances, can be quite tiresome, so if a long uphill climb is involved you use . . .

The herringbone is so named because of the herringbone pattern it leaves on the snow. Basically, the herringbone is a walking step as far as leg, arm, and pole coordination is concerned. The skis are placed at an angle to the direction in which you are going and the ankles are rolled in slightly to put the skis on their inside edges. This prevents the skis from slipping back when walking uphill. The key to the maneuver is to get an adequate but not excessive angle when placing the ski on the snow and making a complete and swift transfer of weight to that ski before taking the next step.

Your first real sliding maneuvers will be straight downhill running and traversing. For both it is important to develop a sound basic stance, shown in the photo above. The weight is resting slightly on the balls of the feet, and ankles are flexed enough so that the knees are just over the toes of the boots. The upper body is bent slightly at the waist.

In straight downhill running on a gentle slope, you sink and rise and rock slightly backward and forward so that you develop mobility and a sense of balance. In traversing you're going across the hill. To prevent the skis from slipping sideways, the skis must be put on edge and most of the weight must be carried on the downhill ski. To accomplish this, the knees are rolled into the hill —that is, toward the uphill side of the hill—and to compensate for this, the upper body is tilted slightly sideways, down the hill.

The kickturn is a good maneuver for turning around when you are in a tight spot and don't want to take chances. Don't try to rush it. Before starting a kickturn either find a level spot or put the skis across the hill so that they won't slide. Make sure you have adequate support from your poles and only then kick the downhill leg up so that the tail of the ski rests on the snow. Move your pole so that is is planted above your uphill ski and out of the way when you, next, pivot the ski on its tail so that it points in the new direction. When the pivoting ski is firmly on the snow and edged, bring the other ski around so that it is parallel to and pointing in the same direction as the pivoted ski.

How do you slow down? On gentle slopes a snowplow will do the job. When you are first learning this maneuver, get into a snowplow from a stationary position by pushing the tails of your skis out so that they form an inverted V. As you push out, put the skis on their inside edges. Then push off down the hill, regulating your speed by changing the angle of the skis and the amount of edging; the greater the angle and the more the skis are on edge, the slower you will go. Once you get the feel of it, you can get into the snowplow from a straight running position by gradually sliding the tails of the skis out and, of course, at the same time, putting the skis on their inside edges. To get out of the snowplow, simply relax the pressure you are putting on the skis with your heels and let the skis run together. Opening and closing the skis as you are coming down the hill is a good exercise not only for mastering the snowplow, but also for mastering the basic elements of edge control.

1 2 3 4

The snowplow turn is favored by beginners because its triangular base provides a stable position during the turn. To get into the turn, start off in a straight snowplow and gradually shift your weight to the ski that will be on the outside of the turn—that is, if you're turning left, transfer your weight to the right ski. As the skis begin to turn, increase the amount of edging on the outside of the ski and decrease the edging on the inside ski. This can be done by moving both knees toward the inside of the turn, as can be seen by comparing photos 2 and 3. As the skis come across the hill, you can simply go into a traverse and stop. Instead of stopping, however, shift your weight to your other ski (the one that's now the uphill ski) and turn in the opposite direction. Don't forget to increase the edging on the outside ski while decreasing it on the inside ski. Failure to do this is the major cause of ragged snowplow turns.

The stem turn. If you think you see a resemblance to the snowplow you're absolutely right. But there's an important difference: Only one ski is pushed out into the V formation. Follow this one through: Starting from a traverse, slide the uphill ski out to the side, at the same time putting the ski on its inside edge. When you've achieved the desired angle, shift your weight to the outside ski. The skis will start to turn. To keep the skis turning, keep your weight on the outside ski. As you pass through the fall line (when the skis are pointing straight downhill), increase the edging on the outside ski and release the edge on the inside ski, just as in the snowplow. As the skis come across the hill again, let the skis run together so that they are parallel to each other as you go into the traverse. Repeat in the opposite direction. Many ski school touch only lightly on the stem turn because it is so closely related to the stem christie.

To sideslip you need a steep slope. Start off with about 70 per cent of your weight resting on the downhill ski. To start slipping, gradually release the edges by rolling the knees away from the hill. A tip: If the uphill ski seems to drag as you are slipping, press slightly with your uphill little toe.

A stem christie starts out much like a stem turn. The uphill ski is slipped out to the side so that it is pointed in the direction of the turn and at the same time it is put on its inside edge. Weight is shifted to the outside ski. However, as the skis start to turn, instead of leaving them in the V position, the inside ski is brought alongside and parallel to the outside ski and the turn is completed with the skis parallel. Note that in this version of the stem christie, up-motion is used to *unweight* the skis. This unweighting makes the skis easier to turn.

Parallel turns are the dream of every beginner. They're safer and faster but they require careful co-ordination of several movements—unweighting both skis, a change of the edges, and turning the skis. In preparation for the turn you first sink slowly and then rise swiftly. As you come to the top of the rise, the skis become light or unweighted; they may even come off the snow if the motion is emphatic enough. At that moment you change from the edges you were riding (the right ones in this case) to the edges that will be toward the inside of the turn (the left ones in this case) and turn the skis slightly. The small amount of initial turning is sufficient to make the skis come around because of fricton and the shape of the skis. The radius of the turn is controlled by edging—the more edging, the sharper the turn will be. Keep the weight on the outside ski. To do this, it is necessary to *angulate*—that is, to lean the upper body to the outside of the turn.

For added stability and more punch to the turn, particularly on steeper terrain, the parallel turn with pole plant is an essential tool of the good skier. A decisive pole plant acts like a trigger to the explosive turn that follows. The pole should be planted slightly to the front and to the side. The result is a tremendous unweighting which gives time to change the edges and the direction of the skis. The resulting change of direction can be extremely sharp. On steep and bumpy slopes, it may be necessary to actually hop the skis off the snow so that they don't get hung up on the terrain above them as they are being turned. The parallel turn with pole plant is far from being the end of skiing maneuvers, but with the fundamentals covered up to this point it is possible to ski anywhere.

All right, so how long *does* it take to learn to ski? The chances are, you will be snowplowing down the beginner's slope by the end of your second day, maybe sooner if you are athletic. Probably ten lessons will go by before you will be capable of a competent stem christie. During those ten lessons you will become familiar not only with the fundamentals of skiing, but you will also be exposed to progressively more difficult terrain. The function of ski instruction is more than teaching you mechanical skills. It is also supposed to build your confidence, and that may be more important than the mere matter of knowing how. If you can approach each new step with confidence, half your job is done.

But simply because your family has learned to ski, don't forget instruction completely. It's a good idea to take a lesson at the beginning of the season to make sure that no one has developed bad habits. A lesson is also indicated when any member of the family is faced with unfamiliar skiing conditions, such as ice or deep powder snow, or when first skiing on a large, unfamiliar mountain. All of you will have more fun this way.

4

SPECIAL PROBLEMS OF CHILDREN

Children take to skiing like the proverbial ducks to water. Unlike adults, whose skiing progress is frequently retarded by a variety of hang-ups—physiological, psychological and social —children have the happy knack of approaching skiing as just another way of having fun. If they are having fun, they'll keep on skiing. If they're not, they'll quit. For most of them it is as simple as that.

Basically, the responsibility of parents is to make sure that their children have fun on skis. This requires proper equipment and clothing, of course, but it also takes some thought on how your child fits into the skiing scheme of things. As noted in the opening chapter, different skiing skills require different types of terrain, and, unless the ski area is a small one, there is a strong tendency for the various members of the family to scatter all over the mountain. There is no harm in this as such, but it may require some organization to cope with the special problems of children.

Although every family seems to have its own way of classifying its children, there are three stages through which the skiing child goes, and each stage has its own manifestations. Age is a factor in each of these stages, but the passage from one stage to the next can differ greatly from child to child, even within a family. It is not at all unusual to see a six-year-old ski a big, difficult mountain with all the assurance of a seasoned pro, but don't be surprised if it takes junior until his teens to really find his skiing groove. Some children improve in all but invisible increments. Others develop with startling suddenness—almost from one ski trip to the next. This does not mean that parents must stand idly by waiting for their children to find their niche in skiing. All kinds of things help a child achieve skiing progress. However, it does require a good deal of understanding and patience. Pushing a child beyond his inclinations of the moment is a good way to spoil his skiing fun.

To start at the beginning, tots present the most difficult problem for skiing parents—so difficult that some families with very young children drop out of skiing until their children are at an age they consider old enough to participate in the sport. Whether dropping out is really necessary is an individual matter for parents to decide. It should be pointed out, however, that the intense construction of ski areas in the last decade has put skiing within easy driving distance of most population

Toddlers require constant attention and care while on the ski slopes.

Falling in the snow can be fun. Many children go through a stage in which they fall deliberately.

Sometimes it is enough just to give them a bit of physical support at the start and then they'll pick up the rest by imitation.

centers in the snowbelt, and that many of these areas provide some sort of baby-sitting service at reasonable cost. In other words, it is possible to get in some skiing when the children are in their infancy without totally disrupting family routine.

More crucial is the question: "How old is old enough to start skiing?" and there are enough different opinions on the subject to fill this book several times over.

No matter how seriously you as an adult take skiing, from a tot's point of view skiing is a game. In introducing him to skiing, keep this in mind. Snow is great fun to slide on, roll around in, and to make snowmen with. It is also cold, and some children, even when dressed warmly, have a negative reaction when first exposed to snow. The only way to find out how a child will react is to expose him to some snowplay as soon as he can walk. A trip outside around the house, broken up by a game or two, will do. If he seems to enjoy this, he is probably ready for 12- to 18-inch skis, which you can make yourself if you have an inclination that way, or which you can buy from a sporting goods or department store for less than $5.

You can get the child started by letting him shuffle around in the snow and by taking him on little walks. After he gains some proficiency in that, you can familiarize him with the sliding sensation by pushing or pulling him along. The next step is to introduce him to a gentle slope and gradually get him used to sliding freely under his own momentum. Be sure to pick a slope that has a flat on the bottom so that the child can coast to a stop. If such a slope is not available, be prepared to catch the child in your arms. One parent can take him up the slope, while the other waits for him below.

One thing you will not have to worry about is the consequences of a fall. Tots tumble all the time and are used to it. The snow is soft, and the skis are so small and loosely attached that there is no way for them to exert any leverage on the child's small legs. If there is any concern, it is likely to be that falling in the snow is so much fun for the child that it will be difficult to get him to do much else.

After a child has learned to slide down the hill under his own power, probably not too much will happen for some time after that. To keep him "skiing" when he is only two or three years

There are numerous games youngsters can play on snow. If they seem to tire of instruction, let them go off by themselves. They'll enjoy the sport more.

old is merely a question of finding a suitably gentle slope where he can slide around and where he has an opportunity to play in the snow. You may encounter some problems if he is ready to learn to turn before he is four years old. Equipment suitable for advanced tots is hard to find and you may have to improvise to get what you want (see the equipment section of this chapter).

Once it appears that your child is ready for turns, remember that young children learn primarily by imitation and that skiing is no exception. There is absolutely no point in telling a tot what to do. You have to set an example and give him a chance to imitate you. Many children have no difficulty in copying their elders once a demonstration has been made. Others may require something more graphic. Children of this type are best taught by having them ski between your skis as you are snow-plow turning down the hill. If you don't feel up to this, have a capable friend or instructor do it for you.

Once a child is turning, your worries about your child's technical progress are over. He may seem to be violating every skiing rule in the book, but actually he isn't, considering his physical development. If he gets sufficient exposure to skiing in the years that follow he will pick up all the fine points as he becomes physiologically capable of doing them. If occasionally you feel that his progress is lagging, the way to correct the situation is not to lecture him on the fine points of ski technique, but to expose him to a situation where his peers are obviously doing better than he is. This is usually enough to spur him on.

Although a tot may become quite capable technically, he will remain in the realm of tot-dom at the very least until he has learned to cope with bathroom problems. The tot's situation is somewhat complicated by the fact that it's more difficult to extract yourself out of a snow suit than out of ordinary clothes. Even though a child is toilet-trained and perfectly capable of taking care of himself under ordinary circumstances, he may need assistance for a year or two longer on the ski slopes. In other words, he may need full-time supervision in skiing even though he is otherwise self-sufficient. Until he is fully capable of taking care of himself, you should stay within shouting distance.

A somewhat more complex problem with tots is their reaction to cold. Within reason, cold as such does no harm. However, caution is required because small children cannot warm up merely by increasing their activity. Once they are cold, they'll stay cold even to the point of physical pain. The only way to cure the situation is to bring the child indoors, warm him up in front of a fire and feed him hot chocolate.

Since it is almost inevitable that children will get cold and since children differ widely in their reactions to the cold, you will have to judge when enough is enough. Usually, children who are getting cold lose their sparkle quite a while before they get cold to the point of pain. Any sign of flagging enthusiasm is usually a good signal that it's time to move indoors.

Don't be alarmed if your youngster falls. Most falls are harmless plops in the snow.

Tots who've had a fairly early start in skiing are usually quite self-sufficient—they can take care of their own bathroom problems and know when to come in from the cold—by the time they are five or six. Usually, by that time they have learned to ride a tow or lift and the only complication remaining is putting on boots and taking care of equipment. Lacing and relacing boots is usually too complicated a chore for a youngster—which is why many parents of young skiers turn to buckle boots—and he has to learn not to leave his skis and poles where he happens to take them off. Your own good example will help in this respect and your insistence that he properly rack his skis and remember where they are will reinforce it.

It should be noted that a considerable number of ski authorities question the value of introducing small children to skiing before they are five. They claim it is a waste of your skiing time to spend hours and hours teaching your child rudimentary maneuvers which he can learn in a matter of days when he is five without handicapping his future progress. It is better, these skeptics say, to put the child in the nursery and maintain your own enthusiasm by skiing on trails suitable to your skill.

This argument is not totally without merit. Teaching a tot to ski and then supervising his activities until he is self-sufficient does take time and it can be bothersome. However, as recent educational research shows, tots are capable of benefiting from various educational experiences at a much earlier age than previously thought. Furthermore, it is one of the few opportunities you have of teaching your child a specific skill without resorting to outside assistance. Granted, what you teach your child is rudimentary by adult standards, but it is perfectly adequate for his needs. And inasmuch as it allows him to play with his parents at an age when there is a rather sharp distinction between adult and child activities, it cannot help but strengthen the family relationship. The chance is never quite as good again.

Starting a child out on skis at age five or six has, as noted, the advantage of reducing the time it takes for him to learn the

If one youngster in a family starts to ski, inevitably the others want to join in the fun, no matter how young. Be prepared for this eventuality.

basic maneuvers. The youngster is more fully coordinated, stronger, more capable of resisting the cold, and better able to take care of himself. The major drawbacks are primarily psychological and every year that you delay after your youngster is about five tends to aggravate them.

If you start your child in what I call the youngster (or grade school) stage, the procedure can be fundamentally the same as with a tot except that the approach can be more direct and vigorous. The chances are the child will have had some experience with snow and cold. And if you ski, he will undoubtedly be aware of it and will probably be anxious to do as his parents do. A set of skis for Christmas or for his birthday is usually sufficient to motivate him to try skiing.

A major difficulty in teaching a six-year-old is the fact that by the time he has reached that age he is quite conscious of the fact he is not supposed to fall and have accidents. You have undoubtedly told him numerous times to watch where he is going and to be careful. When he realizes that it is easy to fall on skis, and it happens in front of you, he may get quite timid until you demonstrate to him—maybe with some falls of your own—that falling is part of the skiing game.

Although you may think that five- and six-year-olds live in a world totally of their own making, you'd be surprised how aware they are of how their peers are skiing. Youngsters frequently get quite discouraged because some playmates ski better than they do. Unfortunately, particularly among parents who know something about skiing, there is a tendency to look for a technical solution—in the way he does his snowplows or whatever—and to ignore the psychological aspect. Usually there is nothing technically wrong and reviving his flagging enthusiasm is simply a matter of restoring his self-confidence. This can be done by working with him alone, away from his friends, until he "recovers." Quite frequently, the cause of his loss of confidence is that he was exposed to too steep a slope too suddenly. By taking him to a gentler slope and then gradually working him up to the bigger hill in easy stages, you can usually renew his enthusiasm without getting involved in technical—do this, do that—instruction.

You may also be surprised to find that your youngster resists instruction from you and this is more and more likely as he grows toward his teens. I have no idea why some children are more teacher-oriented than others, but the fact is that some youngsters will take certain types of instruction more readily from a teacher-like figure than from their parents. If your youngster is teacher oriented it is best not to fight it—the result will be frustrating to all involved—but to call in outside help. Fortunately, there is a good deal of it available. Quite a few ski areas have instructors who specialize in teaching small children and some of these children's ski schools double as baby-sitting services. More reasonable in cost—and usually closer to home—are the many children's ski programs conducted by ski clubs and service organizations. You should check around to see if such programs are available in your

One of the charms of skiing is that youngsters can be off on their own if they want to be, even on the biggest mountains. These two tots are off to Aspen Mountain, one of the largest in the United States.

community or at a nearby ski area because, generally speaking, they provide better ski teaching than you can.

The fact that you have to hand your youngster over to a professional instructor or to a children's ski program is absolutely no reflection on your skiing ability. The difference between you and an instructor is that he is trained *and paid* to teach and brings a degree of experience and concentration to his task that even the most willing parent finds difficult to muster. And the better a skier you are, the less likely it will be that you can muster that concentration. Mentally, you'll always

A special section of the ski school is devoted to youngsters five years and older. Instructors make skiing fun and at the same time teach the fundamentals correctly.

be off on your favorite trail, and the result is that you grow impatient with your youngster. He'll quickly sense this impatience and skiing will no longer be fun for him. He'll cry, claim he's cold, or will want to go to the bathroom (or all three) just to get away. It will take a lot of persuasion to get him to come back again.

Again, as in the case of tots, do not expect your youngster to assume the classic stances of skiing, even if he does take lessons. In his state of physical development, he's probably doing what is ideal for him. At least until he is about seven or eight, don't worry about how he looks as long as he can turn and is getting down the hill all right.

Of course, there will be times when he will have trouble, and usually this comes when his legs and body grow toward their ultimate proportions. Because of these physical changes, his technique may no longer be quite adequate for what he is trying to do. A good-humored demonstration of what he is doing wrong will usually correct his problem, although you may have to resort to lessons if it persists.

You should also recognize that your youngster will hit learning plateaus in skiing, just as in everything else. You can help him work his way out of these plateaus by a change of scene, with games, or, if he is sufficiently advanced, by entering him in a children's race. It doesn't do any harm to needle him a little, but excessive pressure should be avoided because he's usually just as anxious that he improve as you are.

As far as I am concerned, a youngster remains a youngster— no matter how good a skier he is—until he is capable of taking care of himself completely. Usually, the last step in this development is when he has developed the strength and know-how to lace his own boots correctly. Lacing boots is no easy chore, particularly for a girl, and it is not at all unusual for a child to need help with this job until he is ten or eleven. Of course, you can short-circuit this problem with buckle boots, but this raises other problems, as you will see in the equipment section of this chapter.

If your children are in their pre-teens or teens before they have a chance to learn to ski, the most effective approach is to

At first you may have to help your youngster get up the ski slope. Later they will do it on their own.

treat them as adults. At this age they want to act like adults anyway, and letting them learn to ski like adults gives them the opportunity.

Whether you should even try to teach your children if they are over ten—the junior stage—depends a great deal on how well you ski. By the time a child has reached this age, he is quick to spot the difference between a good skier and one who is less proficient, and on those grounds he may reject your instruction, even if fundamentally sound. If you are something less than a striking figure on skis, it is best that you leave his instruction to someone who is fully qualified for the job.

Regardless of whether you teach him or not, a child in the junior stage can pose some difficult problems when he is first learning. He is going to be acutely aware that a good many of his contemporaries and many children younger than he are skiing better than he is. Where a youngster is apt to get discouraged, a junior-age beginner is much more likely to get reckless to cover up what in his mind are shortcomings. At the same time, because his body and legs are now beginning to assume adult proportions, he's much more vulnerable to injury. You may have to sit on him severely to keep him from being reckless—schussbooming, as it is called in skiing.

Junior-stage skiers have an additional psychological hazard because they are going through their period of greatest growth and the coordination problems it brings with it. Their rate of real progress is going to be a good deal slower because, very much like an adult who learns to ski, they have to overcome fears of height, speed, accidents and injuries, and their acute self-consciousness. One of the best ways to help a child in that stage is to make sure that he gets plenty of physical exercise in addition to his skiing. A great many of the so-called coordination problems are simply lack of good physical condition.

Fortunately, children in the junior stage are amenable to reason. If their first few times on skis are less than a roaring success they can recognize that there is an ultimate reward for their efforts. They will still become frustrated and impatient, but usually it is enough for you to point out that bad

If a child shows signs of becoming reckless—always possible in so exciting a sport as skiing—enroll him in an advanced children's class where the fast skiing is properly supervised.

attitudes in skiing are usually self-defeating. Pointing out that he is not the only one with troubles will teach him to laugh at himself and restore his ambition.

CLOTHING FOR CHILDREN

An adult can write off his investment in ski clothing and equipment over several years and thereby justify its cost. A child's outfit does not lend itself to the same cost rationale. He will outgrow it long before he has worn it out. If you have several children, this can be a major consideration in deciding whether you and they will ski or not.

Yet it is important that children have good clothing and equipment. You cannot ski with boots that give no support and with skis that have bad edges. Don't expect your child to be any different. Improper clothing and equipment can badly handicap his skiing.

Getting good ski clothing for a child is the least of the problems. As noted in Chapter 3, his ski clothing can be part of his winter wardrobe at very little extra cost, and, unless your child is growing exceptionally fast, can be fitted in such a way that it can be worn for two seasons. If he has any problems with clothing at all it is usually caused by overconcern on your part. Rightfully, you are concerned that he will get cold—and he will. But bundling him up in clothes is not the answer. Swaddling the child in mufflers and sweaters and other bulky clothing will merely immobilize him physically without making him any warmer or enabling him to endure the cold longer. The only way to keep a young child warm is to bring him indoors periodically and warm him up.

There are two key items in the child's wardrobe whose importance is frequently overlooked: hat and mittens. In a child particularly, more body heat is lost through the head than any other part of the body. This loss of body heat is first felt in the hands.

In buying hats and mittens for children, keep in mind that they must not only keep body heat in, but must also be able to

This youngster is properly garbed—note mittens and parka with built-in hood—to brave the ski slopes.

shed snow readily. Once hats and mitten get wet, they are use-
less. They then conduct body heat rather than keeping it in.
For this reason plain wool mittens and, if the child still falls
quite a bit, wool hats are not suitable for skiing. Mitten should
have a liner of wool or other insulating material and should be
covered with leather or a combination of leather and nylon
so that they can shed the snow. (The child will need such
mittens anyway once he starts riding the rope tow.) Since most
hats are wool, they should be covered with a nylon hood. Most
ski parkas have hoods built in and you should make sure your
child's parka has this feature when you are buying one.

If possible, have spare mittens and hats with you. Hats and
mittens are the items most frequently lost. Have the extras on
hand not only as replacements, but as substitutes in case the
others get wet.

EQUIPMENT FOR CHILDREN

The child's equipment needs are not resolved quite as easily.
Good equipment at a reasonable price is hard to find, and it
may take considerable shopping around to find what you need.
Fortunately, because of these problems, skiers have devised all
kinds of mechanisms to resolve the issue.

You can rent children's equipment both by the day and by
the season. For families that ski fairly frequently—eight to ten
days a year, or more—the latter proposition is particularly
attractive because the child can be equipped for his needs of
the moment without concern about his needs for the following
year. Seasonal rentals run between $30 and $45 a season, and
the outfit you get for this money is invariably far superior to
anything you might buy at twice the cost. Unfortunately, seasonal rental of children's equipment is not yet universal. Furthermore, if more than three children are involved, the cost
may be on the steep side.

But regardless of whether you rent or buy, but particularly
if you buy, you should be aware of what constitutes good children's equipment. If you are going to take advantage of ski
swaps, or plan to buy and sell used equipment, or expect to

hand the equipment down to a younger child, this knowledge is invaluable.

As with adults, *boots* are usually the young skier's major problem. As long as the child is in the snow-play stage, his skis can be rigged in such a way that he can use his rubber boots. And if he skis on gentle slopes, he can get away with simple rubber ski boots costing between $7 and $10. Once he advances beyond these stages, he will need boots which give a great deal more support. Anything good along these lines is going to cost between $20 and $30.

Although there is some debate on this, it is possible to fit boots so that they will last two years. Children's feet grow faster in length than in width and buying boots a size larger than needed will do no harm as long as the boots fit well around the heels and ankles. However, it is not good practice to buy boots so large that it takes more than two pairs of socks

If you like to ski yourself you will have to teach the children to take care of themselves.

to make them fit snugly. The extra year you think you gain will be lost anyway because a poorly fitted boot will wrinkle and sag and will be uncomfortable by the time your child grows into it.

Aside from the fact that good boots are going to be warmer and more comfortable, they have the big advantage of retaining their value in the various used equipment markets if they have had good maintenance. Good boots, particularly in the smaller sizes, are hard to find and can be readily sold or traded.

While good boots for children up to about ten find a ready market, the boot problem is going to become steadily more complex as the youngster grows toward his teens. Up to about the age of ten, a child's skiing activity is not vigorous enough to break down a good boot, even with fairly heavy participation. This is frequently not the case with children over ten. Many become extremely hard on boots at this age and good ($30 to $40 in junior sizes) may not be good enough. Renting for the season may be the best solution even though it is somewhat more expensive (about $15 to $20 a year). Also, explore the extremely sturdy plastic boots. These boots are just beginning to come on the market and at this writing are available only in the $50 to $100 category. However, it is safe to predict that they will soon appear in a wider range of prices. Because these boots do not break down as leather boots do, they should retain a high resale or trade-in value, making them ideal for use by growing youngsters—once they are available at prices less than astronomic.

At this point, generally speaking, lace boots are better for children than buckle boots. Lace boots not only cost less (about $10 less for an equivalent buckle model), but are far easier to fit. Furthermore, buckle boots have to be fitted in such a way that it is only rarely possible to get more than one season's use out of them. However, they do have the advantage of convenience. Few children can lace their own boots properly before they are eight or nine, and if you have to lace and relace several pairs of children's boots on every ski outing you may decide that the convenience outweighs the cost.

If you buy children's boots with the idea of recovering part of their cost through trading in or resale, good maintenance is essential. This calls for keeping the boots in a boot press when they are not in use, periodic application of special ski boot polish and sole sealer (if the boots don't have a "sealed" or "molded" sole), and making sure that your child uses his boots only for skiing. This latter point can be critically important since in snow play (other than skiing) boot soles can be easily curled. Boots whose soles are not flat lose a good deal of their resale value.

As with adult boots, it does not pay, either in terms of skiing fun or foot health and comfort, to scrimp on children's ski boots. If you are on budget restrictions, do your best with boots, then cut corners on the rest of the equipment.

Once your youngster moves out of the snow-play stage, he will need *bindings* which will hold the boots tightly to the skis. The best approach is to start him off with a good releasable binding. Granted, tots and youngsters are flexible enough to take twists and tangles which would shatter the legs of even a well-conditioned adult. But unlike all other children's equipment and clothing, a child does not outgrow his bindings until he weighs about 100 pounds, which, in the case of some girls, may be never. An investment of $15 to $20 will buy the best children's bindings available and may well prevent that one-in-a-million accident.

Once the bindings have been adjusted, you can fix the setting with lock-screw compound (available in most hardware stores) so that he cannot change the setting. And, of course, you should check the setting periodically to make sure that it has not changed for other reasons.

Skis do not present any particular problem. Although the general rule is that skis should be no longer than the child is tall until he learns to ski something that approaches parallel, this is not especially critical. A couple of inches one way or another will not make much difference.

The only area of difficulty is a technical one. It is difficult to make a flexible short-length wood ski that is not excessively

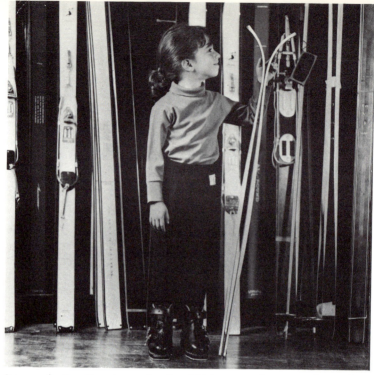

Proper selection of equipment for the child is a must. Boots are of special importance. Skis should be as long as the child is tall, but can vary a couple of inches one way or the other without making too much difference.

fragile. Manufacturers compensate for this stiffness by reducing the amount of camber, but this may not be enough if you have a lightweight youngster. Be sure that he can flatten the skis out when his weight is distributed equally on both skis. If the skis are too stiff, he will have difficulty in turning.

In making a selection, your choices for all practical purposes will boil down to wood skis for tots and youngsters under seven, to wood and metal skis for children between eight and their teens, and to wood, metal and plastic skis from the teens on.

What was said in Chapter 3 about the pros and cons of wood, metal and plastic skis, applies equally to children's skis. Wood skis cost the least ($10 to $60), but are subject to warpage and breakage; metal skis are the most durable; and plastic skis for a growing teenager are a dubious luxury at this point.

In shopping for wood skis, you will find everything from the most primitive to the ultrasophisticated. Rock-bottom prices will get you very little, but for between $15 and $20 you will get a laminated ski with good steel edges and a plastic base that will need waxing only when the snow is damp or wet. For $5 to $10 more, you can get such features as plastic top edges, polyethylene bottoms, and tip and tail protectors, and for another $10 the ski will be encased in protective plastic. The latter feature will keep the ski looking nicer longer, but it means that it cannot be refinished as a ski with wooden surfaces can. If you are a do-it-yourselfer, you may be able to recover a greater percentage of your purchase price with skis without this feature than with it.

The cost of children's skis goes up as their length increases —about $5 for every six inches—until they reach adult costs in middle-teen sizes. As children approach this point, parents usually begin to think in terms of metal skis, in large part because they may have encountered the breakage problem of wood skis.

All consideration of cost aside for a moment, the advantage of metal skis for children is that they can be designed to be extremely flexible without sacrifice of either strength or durability. The biggest disadvantage is the high initial cost (at least $75 if the ski comes with a good warranty) and the relatively limited usage (three years at the most) that a child can get from a pair. This is partially offset by the higher resale or trade-in value of metal skis (50 per cent of purchase price is not unusual). However, it is doubtful if the per-year cost of metal skis will ever be as low as wood skis, even when the possibility of breakage is considered. Unless your child is particularly hard on wood skis, it is safe to say that the net per-year cost of metal skis is going to run $5 to $10 higher than that of wood skis. Of course, you may decide that the more suitable skiing characteristics and the relatively maintenance-free nature of metal skis make this extra cost worth it. But you should weigh this fact against the more critical boot requirements.

Ski poles are another noncritical area of ski equipment. Tots and youngsters who are in the beginning stages need them only for walking and there is a school of thought that maintains they shouldn't use them at all when skiing downhill.

In any event, children's poles are not a budget-cracking item. They are available in prices ranging from $3.50 to $15, but it is only rarely that you have to go over $10. For small children, tonkin cane or bamboo poles will do. Once they improve and grow older, they will need something more rigid, which means something of aluminum alloy tubing. The size criterion is the same as for adults—they should pass easily under the armpit—but no great harm is done if they are a little longer.

After reading this chapter you may well ask yourself if the trouble you take to teach your children to ski and to equip them properly is really worth it, particularly if they are very young.

The answer as far as I am concerned is *yes,* and I am sure that an overwhelming majority of parents of young skiers will agree with me. Except for the initiation period, children can ski on a par with adults. They are not handicapped by size, weight, strength, education, or score. There are few family activities where one or more of these factors do not come into play. Skiing, being one of the exceptions, is well worth cultivating in your children. It will give them a lifetime of pleasure.

5

SAFETY IN SKIING...IT'S UP TO YOU

There's no way around it, skiing is a *potentially* hazardous sport. This is not necessarily a drawback. I suspect that one of the major reasons for the increasing popularity of skiing is that it does involve some extraordinary risks which test our courage and our judgment of nature.

But simply because the risks exist, it is not necessary to succumb to them. To the contrary, the whole purpose of taking a risk is to surmount it . . . intact. To do so requires an appreciation of the risks involved in an acivity and to find ways to minimize them. As well as seeking to minimize the risks, you should also seek to minimize the costs in case an accident does happen. In many cases your health and accident policy covers skiing accidents. If it does not, the United States Ski Association, which may be joined through your local ski club, offers ski accident insurance on both an individual and a family basis at very reasonable cost.

There are all kinds of risks in skiing, and this chapter will touch briefly on them. However, the biggest single risk is the simple act of skiing! A skier charges down a mountain with two boards on his feet, a combination that can exert a leverage on muscles, tendons, bones, and joints beyond their ability to withstand. Leg, knee, and ankle injuries are the most common of ski injuries.

The way to avoid these injuries is to avoid giving the skis the opportunity to exert this leverage on your legs. The most obvious way is to avoid falling, hardly a practical solution, especially for those who are less than expert. Knowing how to fall helps, but since not all falls can be anticipated, this bit of knowledge is only of limited use.

Based on experiments, one of the most satisfactory ways to avoid injury is to be in good physical condition. As noted in the previous chapter, good physical condition speeds up your learning process tremendously, in itself an important factor in avoiding injury, but equally important is that you don't tire as readily. A tired skier is more likely to get himself into an injury-producing situation, not so much because of lack of strength, but because of loss of coordination. And, of course, good physical condition enables your muscles to take far greater stresses before they give.

Good physical condition is essential for skiing safety. Competitors start training in late summer or early fall, long before snow is on ground. Although pleasure skiers don't go to the length competitors do, to be in good shape greatly enhances their enjoyment of skiing.

How can you get in shape? I, personally, don't have too much faith in exercise regimes of any kind, although they may be necessary if you've let yourself slip. In exercising for skiing, emphasis should be given to strengthening and limbering up leg and abdominal muscles. You can achieve this condition by doing the standard fitness exercises such as sit-ups, push-ups, toe-touching, leg-lifts, and jogging. Better still, get yourself and your family into an exercise class where competition will spur you on; at home you can goof off too easily without anyone being the wiser. Many ski clubs and most YMCA's in the ski regions of this country hold such classes.

If your children take gym classes regularly, there's probably no need to worry about their physical condition. If you are in doubt, it might be wise to have them take a physical fitness test and to have them checked over by your family physician. Usually, the promise of skiing is enough to spur them on during their school exercise periods.

One of the major handicaps most people face in conditioning is excess weight. An overweight person finds it hard to exercise and for that reason tends to avoid it. The result is that he gains more weight . . . and so on and on . . . unless he makes a deliberate effort to break the circle. One of the strong pluses for skiing is that it provides the motivation for many to break out of this vicious circle.

Good physical condition can provide a remarkable amount of protection against injury. You can further minimize the risks by outfitting yourself and your family with *good, properly adjusted* release bindings. The emphasis is on *good* because not all bindings work consistently well, and on *properly adjusted* because even the best binding will not work if its release features are inoperative for any one of several reasons.

Fortunately, most of the well-known brands of bindings are well known precisely because they have accumulated a record of reliability. Proper adjustment is something else again because it is the responsibility of the skier to make sure the bindings are functioning.

Life would be a great deal simpler and safer if binding adjustment were not necessary. But there are so many variables, it's impossible for one setting to take them all into account. Although manufacturers are making constant progress in improving their product, the educational process to take maximum advantage of these improvements is still lagging badly.

For the binding to work properly, the basic factors are involved: correct mounting, proper adjustment, and careful maintenance.

Mounting bindings is a fairly critical operation and should be done by a qualified ski repair shop. The usual $5 to $10 mounting fee may seem a bit steep, but is well worth it.

Each brand of bindings has its own adjustment peculiarities. It is absolutely essential that you read with care the instructions that come with the bindings. If you are to make the

Skis, boots and bindings should be properly adjusted to the needs of each member of your family. In the picture, a store clerk is using the Lipe Release Check to determine the release setting of a binding. A portable model is available for use by skiers.

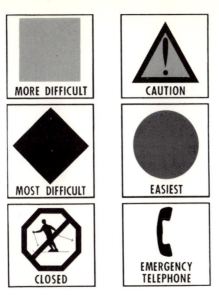

These trail signs perform the same function in ski areas that traffic signs do on the highways. They tell you where you should and shouldn't be and warn you of hazards. Remember that one mountain's easiest trail may well compare with another mountain's most difficult. Also keep in mind that conditions can change. The easiest slope on a mountain can sometimes become extremely difficult.

most of their releasing features, you must know how they operate, how they are reset after they release, how to adjust them, and how to maintain them. If you cannot understand the instructions, get an explanation from your ski shop before you go skiing.

Adjusting by sight or feel is possible, but not especially accurate except in the case of a heel or cable release. The only way to get a precise adjustment is with an instrument— some sort of torque-indicating device, or with a Lipe Release Check, which is made specifically for this purpose. Most ski shops have a bench model. It is also available in a small, portable model for use by skiers for about $20. There is no better investment, particularly since the instructions that come with the device cover all aspects of proper adjustment in easy-to-understand language.

In almost all cases, the procedure for getting the bindings into proper adjustment may be a bit cumbersome, but getting the adjustment right is more than worth the trouble. Combined with good physical condition, this can eliminate all but a minute percentage of all ski injuries.

Although good condition and properly adjusted bindings will protect in most injury-producing situations, they are not 100 per cent foolproof. They should not be a substitute for good judgment. Good judgment in skiing requires that you know the meaning of the trail signs and the degrees of difficulty that they represent and the dangers of which they warn. Good judgment requires that you know that the degree of difficulty increases when trails and slopes become icy or are covered with deep snow. Good judgment requires that you know that flat light reduces visibility and also your ability to discriminate between various terrain features. And good judgment requires that you treat other skiers with courtesy and respect so that you don't produce a potentially dangerous situation.

A most important contribution to skiing safety is slope grooming. By packing out the slopes, ski areas make skiing a great deal easier for inexperienced skiers. If you haven't learned how to handle deep snow or ice, stay on the groomed portions of the slope.

Most safety considerations in skiing are a matter of every-day common sense plus a little experience. However, there are three areas of safety which require special precautions: Lift riding, frost bite and avalanches.

Lift riding. There are seven basic types of lifts in use throughout North America, all but two of which require that you get "aboard" while the lift is in motion. This is easy enough for the skier who has gone through the loading and riding procedure. If you are not familiar with a particular kind of lift be sure to read the instructions posted at the lift terminal and observe the list of don'ts scrupulously. These instructions and don'ts vary both between different types of lifts and between lifts of the same type and there is little point in detailing them here. However, some general rules do apply. In drag-type lifts—those that pull you along on the snow—do not ski out of the prepared track, and when you get off let go of the bar or rope easily. In aerial lifts—those that lift you above the ground—avoid anything that will cause the chair or cabin to bounce up and down. Failure to observe these basic rules is the cause of the vast majority of lift accidents.

Frostbite. Although skiing is a cold-weather sport, frostbite is a surprisingly minor factor in skiing. Because skiers are aware of this, there is a tendency to get careless about this hazard.

The major problem with frostbite is that the skier who has it is not aware that he does have it. Just one of the reasons why you should never ski alone is that a companion can readily spot frostbite when the affected area begins to turn grayish-white. If caught in time—simply warm up the frost-bitten spot gently—there are no serious consequences. If the frostbite is prolonged, however, the affected area will at the very least be almost permanently sensitive to cold, and extreme cases may require some sort of surgery, although this is extremely rare in skiing. Prevention is simply a matter of being on guard.

Avalanches. Avalanches represent a danger of an entirely different magnitude. Fatalities in skiing are relatively rare con-

There are exceptions to almost every rule about avalanches. Touring skiers and those who ski deep powder must take avalanches into account.

sidering that there are over two million skiers, but the majority of those that do occur are caused by avalanches.

People who have spent a lifetime studying avalanches are the first to admit that every so-called rule about avalanches has frequent exceptions. Almost any steep slope can slide. This need not worry the skier who skis on heavily skied slopes within a ski area, but touring skiers and those who like to ski deep powder must take the avalanche factor into consideration.

There is no room here, nor is it within the province of this book, to go into all the complex aspects of avalanches. Skiers who venture into avalanche terrain should be experienced skiers, or at the very least should be accompanied by skiers who do possess a thorough knowledge of avalanche problems and procedures. For those who want further information, "Snow Avalanches," Agriculture Handbook No. 64 is available from the Superintendent of Documents, U.S. Government Printing Office, Washington, D.C. 20402, for 60 cents. It is an excellent treatment of the subject. Those not willing to go to this trouble should not venture into avalanche terrain.

Finally, suppose that, despite all the precautions, you or one of the members of your family is injured and cannot continue to the bottom of the slope.

The first step is to fight the feeling of panic which is the inevitable aftermath of a serious injury. To use the vernacular, keep your cool. This goes for both the injured skier and his companions, particularly the latter.

The ski patrol is composed of expert skiers adept at first aid. The men of the patrol take over and do an excellent job when accidents occur on the ski slopes.

The second step is to assess the nature of the injury to the best of your ability. If you know first aid, by all means use it, particularly if blood is involved. The chances are that it will be a leg that is injured, but don't automatically assume that this is so. It could be something else, and this may have a bearing on your next step. In all cases, remember that the basic principles of first aid apply. If you do not know what you are doing, limit yourself to making the victim warm and comfortable.

If it is possible to remove the injured skier's skis, do so, providing it can be done without further intensifying his pain. Stick the skis into the snow X fashion about 20 feet above the skier to warn other skiers of the accident. If his skis cannot be easily removed, use your own.

Then call the ski patrol, making sure that you can pinpoint the location of the accident. If possible try to get someone to stay with the skier, or try to get a bystander to call the patrol for you. Do not leave the injured skier alone unless it becomes absolutely essential.

After rendering emergency first aid, the patrol transports the skier to the base area where he can receive medical attention if necessary.

Generally speaking, the patrol needs no extra help to do its job. But stick around anyway, just in case.

The many safety precautions in skiing may sound discouragingly involved. But, like skiing itself, ski safety has to be consciously learned. Once learned, it becomes second nature and no more involved than the safety precautions you take when driving an automobile.

And talking about automobiles, don't forget in going to and from skiing that the highway is a lot more dangerous than the ski slope.

6

WHERE PLANNING PAYS OFF: THE SKI TRIP

Learning to ski is important. Buying good, serviceable equipment for your family and yourself is important. But neither is of any avail unless you also take into account the time and cost involved in your family ski trips. As you make your calculations for the season, budget both time and money for going skiing.

In many families, time is often a more precious commodity than money. Work, school and vacation schedules may be such that there is all too little time for skiing. The very first step in your ski trip planning is to get a calendar and mark all of the days and/or weeks on which ski trips are possible. The next step is to determine how much skiing you can afford. You may wish to figure this out in terms of a total sum per season, so much per month or a certain amount per week.

A key factor in your ski trip costs is accessibility to skiing. If you live in an area where there is snow on the ground all winter long, you are in good shape. A ski trip need not cost you a penny if you tour instead of going to a lift-served area. All that is involved is the time you can spend on your ski outing. (This aspect of skiing will be discussed in more detail in the next chapter.) If you are like most Americans, however, you'll prefer the services of a tow or lift for uphill transportation and you must expect to pay for the convenience.

Where do you find information on ski areas? Your skiing neighbors or your ski shop will help you find something suitable close by. However, if you plan to go further afield, if you need services such as a nursery, or are looking for a special package arrangement, you may have to consult other sources. The ski publications you find on newsstands and in ski shops are helpful and there are a number of ski area guides. The best known of these is *Skiing* magazine's *Ski Area Guide,* which not only lists ski areas and accommodations, but also provides helpful hints on all aspects of travel.

But before we get into elaborate trips, let's take it from the beginning. If you live in an area where there is plenty of snow, you are in good shape. The chances are there will be some sort of ski area close to you. If this area satisfies your desire for challenge and variety, skiing for you and your family can be a very economical affair involving little more than the cost of lift tickets and hot chocolate for your children. You simply jump into your car whenever the mood strikes you.

When you do most of your skiing at one area, particularly when you do a lot of it because it is close and convenient, you should investigate the economies possible with a family season pass. Season pass policies vary from area to area, but most small- and medium-sized areas charge around $100 for the first adult, $50 for the second adult, and from $15 to $25 for each child. Whether a season pass saves you money depends on how much time you have for skiing and whether your crystal ball tells you that it's going to be a good season. Money paid for season tickets is not refunded if there is no snow.

If the snow in your immediate area is marginal or nonexistent, your problem is somewhat more complicated depending on how far you have to travel to reach skiable snow and how much time you have available. Mere absence of snow in your backyard is not necessarily a criterion. There are several major population centers in the United States where snow seldom stays on the ground if it falls at all, yet where good skiing is less than two hours' drive away.

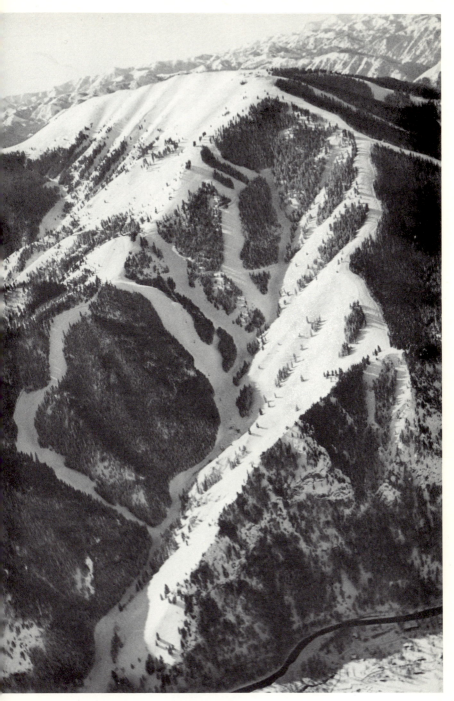

A trip is worthwhile to get to a ski area such as this.

It would be well at this point to make a distinction between the various types of trips. Day skiing is where the party goes and returns the same day. Lunch can be taken along and no overnight stays are involved. For day skiing to be pleasant, driving time should be no more than two hours each way or the maximum travel time you think your children can stand. Weekend or holiday skiing usually involves an overnight stay either at or near an area and meals at the lodge or at a restaurant. Skiers, who admittedly are a hardy crew, think little of traveling anywhere from four to eight hours each way for a weekend of skiing. Vacation skiing involves a week or more of skiing and usually means skiing at one of the larger resorts. How far you go on a ski vacation depends largely on your pocketbook.

In terms of cash outlay, day skiing is probably the most

With modern means of transportation, ski areas are within the reach of almost every skiing family.

economical, particularly if you are in a position to take advantage of a season pass. In contrast, weekend and holiday skiing is the most expensive when you count transportation, lodging, meal and lift ticket costs in relation to the amount of skiing done by you and your family. Not only are prices at a premium, but you'll get a lot less skiing because areas are crowded.

Whenever possible, avoid weekend and holiday skiing. This may be difficult to do if you want to ski at all, but either by judicious bargaining with your employer or by taking advantage of night skiing where it is available, you may be able to surmount the problem. Your skiing dollar goes a lot further with midweek skiing—somewhere on the order of 25 to 50 per cent.

If you cannot avoid weekend and holiday skiing, you can resort to two stratagems which, if they don't necessarily save you cash, at least can give you better value for your money. The better of the two is to ski early and late in the season when skiers don't turn out en masse. The other is to search out smaller, less crowded areas, many of which can be found fairly close to home or in the shadow of the larger, more popular weekend areas. The skiing may be less varied and exciting than on the bigger mountain, but it will keep you in skiing trim until there is time and/or money for a real ski vacation.

Your family's skiing skill and other considerations should also play a role in your ski trip planning. For instance, it makes little sense to go to a big, high-cost area if all you can do is to supervise your youngster as he makes his first snowplow turns. The nearest rope-tow slope is good enough for that. On the other hand, leaving the children at home when you go on a ski vacation may not make much sense either if the baby-sitting charges are going to be higher than the cost of a ski package for a youngster, particularly if this ski package happens to include much-needed ski lessons.

Many families still consider a ski vacation something of a luxury, but with three- and four-week vacations from work becoming more common every year, a week of winter vacation is no longer unusual, even for families of relatively modest means. The question is *when* and *where?*

In the Colorado Rockies, majestic Mt. Hayden, 13,561 feet, looms high above Aspen.

Plans for ski vacations invariably hinge on the children's school schedule. Unfortunately, this schedule rarely coincides with what is most economical and convenient for the skiing family. Ski season breaks usually come over Christmas and New Year's, on Washington's Birthday, and over Easter. All these dates fall within the high season, which means that ski resorts both in the United States and Europe are busy and crowded and charge premium prices for lifts and lodging.

Many skiing families get around this difficulty by ignoring the school schedule and taking their children out of school whenever their ski vacation comes due. (In some highly ski-conscious areas, schools have taken the hint by scheduling a short break during the last part of January or in early February, but these are rare.) The skiing family has the choice either of taking this drastic step or paying the higher prices prevalent during the high season. The decision will have to be yours, but if you are caught in such a bind it will help the cause of skiing tremendously if you point out to your school superintendent that the practice of three-month summer vacations is an anachronism in the middle of the 20th century and that very few children are needed on the farm these days.

You will have to plan your ski vacation well in advance, particularly if you are forced to vacation in high season—more or less officially from December 15 to January 1, from mid-February to mid-March, and Easter week if it falls between mid-March and mid-April. During these periods ski areas and lodges are packed to capacity and unless you get your reservation in early you may have to pay more than you planned on, or you may be shut out completely. The situation is especially critical over Christmas and New Year's.

A skier heads down the slopes of Schweitzer Basin at Sandpoint, Idaho. The lodge and parking lot are visible at bottom of open area.

In planning your ski vacation, shrewd shopping can save you money, even in high season. Most resorts give discounts on three or more days of lifts and lessons, and lodging comes in a large variety of styles and prices. A good many lodges have dormitory-type accommodations in addition to the customary doubles, a point to keep in mind if your family is a fairly large one. There are also varying amounts of food included in the lodging price. European-plan lodges serve only coffee and rolls for breakfast. American-plan lodges (unusual at ski resorts) include all meals in their price. And modified American-plan lodges include breakfast and dinner only. Strangely enough, most European hotels are on full American plan while most lodges at American resorts are on the European plan.

If you have a choice within a given resort, your personal inclination will have to be your guide. Usually, a modified American-plan lodge is the most economical, but if you crave variety of menu or don't want to take a chance on the chef, you are going to be better off with a European-plan lodge.

The best way to find out these details is to write to the resort or resorts of your choice. The reply will bring you one or more folders describing the resort and its facilities. If the resort is a big one, the folder may be skimpy on details of lodges and restaurants. In that case, zero in on those lodges that look most promising to you. They in turn will send you a more detailed folder of what they have to offer. Once you have found what you need, write for a reservation giving dates of arrival and departure, the number of people in your party, and any special needs that you may have. A deposit covering the first and last day of your stay, or of about 25 per cent, will seal the bargain. This deposit can be sent either with your reservation inquiry or when it is requested after your reservation has been made by the lodge.

If the resort of your choice is at some distance, transportation costs and time are additional factors that you will have to take into account. A car is by far the most convenient means of getting to a ski area, particularly if lodging is some distance from the lift. Since this distance has some bearing on the cost of lodges, having a car can save money in more ways than one. However, this convenience and possible saving must be measured against the time element. If your vacation is a short one, you may not want to spend two or three days riding in a car.

When you have to use public transportation, your best bet is to use the service of a travel agent. It costs you nothing, and it can save you large amounts of money. By traveling at certain times, by using various plans—some of which involve lifts, food, and lodging at the resort—and by meeting certain conditions you can travel at a cost considerably below that of the standard fare. Unfortunately for the public, these low-fare programs are almost incomprehensible to anyone other than a specialist and, what's more, they are constantly changing. Hence the need for a travel agent, or at least the travel adviser of an airline.

In making your ski vacation plans you needn't confine yourself to a single resort. For instance, if you live in the East, you can make a rewarding tour of the major New England areas, hitting one a day during the week and staying at a motel on the way from one resort to the next. If you don't mind the daily unpacking and repacking, this type of vacation can be great fun for the variety it makes possible. It also can be quite economical.

When making ski trip plans, you should not overlook the economies and conveniences possible by being affiliated with a ski club. Most ski clubs in areas some distance away from ski regions consider ski trip arrangements their major mission. This can be of tremendous help to the skiing family. Even if you don't take advantage of the trips the club arranges, club members are a good source of all kinds of skiing know-how. And you are almost certain to encounter a kindred soul with much the same problems that you have. Mutual assistance can cut the cost of skiing or at least give your children an opportunity to ski when you are not able to go.

Having decided on a trip, go prepared, even if it is only for a day. You need warm underwear, ski pants, parkas, sweaters, socks, turtlenecks, hats, gloves, goggles or sunglasses, skis, boots, poles, and wax. Keeping all these items in mind may pose no difficulties for yourself, but if you have youngsters you will have to keep inventory for them. Particularly on day trips, where time is of the essence, get ready the night before, then double-check as everyone gets into the car. If any item is missing from the list, one or more people in the group are going to be unhappy—either because of skiing time lost or because of the nick in your pocketbook or both.

Youngsters should learn as soon as possible to take care of their own ski outfits. This means that they not only must make sure they bring everything with them, but also that they bring it back. The sooner they learn these skiing facts of life, the more efficient the operation of transferring the family from home to slope and back again.

If an overnight stay is involved in the trip, don't complicate your life by taking along a lot of "just-in-case" articles. An

Waterville Valley, in New Hampshire, is typical of the eastern ski resorts which can be reached quite easily by the millions of metropolitan residents.

extra set of underwear per person, pajamas, toiletries and perhaps an extra turtleneck are sufficient for weekends. For vacations, merely bring enough underwear and personal articles sufficient for the time of the vacation and add one informal outfit, for variety and change, in addition to the one you'll be wearing on your way to the resort. This may appear to be skimpy, but you won't think so by the time you manhandle skis, boots, poles, and baggage, particularly when you are using public transportation. Getting to a ski resort may involve several changes, and the less gear you have the happier you will be. And rest assured, you won't be underdressed when you get to the resort. Most ski activities are highly informal.

While day and weekend trips confine you to skiing in your own section of the country, ski vacations offer all kinds of possibilities. These are limited only by your ability to pay the transportation costs.

It is not feasible here to give details about any vacation ski

Vail Village looks like a setting in the Tyrol, yet is just 110 miles west of Denver, Colo., in the valley of the Gore mountain range.

areas. For these, read the current and back issues of the various ski publications, particularly *Skiing* magazine, *Ski* magazine, and the *Ski Area Guide*. The latter is particularly helpful because it provides capsule reports on the top areas and such essential basic information as addresses, telephone numbers, and a listing of the facilities. More than a thousand areas are listed in the directory.

In addition to American areas, don't overlook the excellent and very reasonable skiing available in Canada. Canada's major ski regions are similar to our own and you won't feel like a lost soul if you cross the border. Of course, the European Alpine countries—Switzerland, Austria, France, and Italy—are considered to be the ultimate, and once you've paid the fare to Europe, very reasonable by our standards. There is also quite a bit of skiing in the Southern Hemisphere—in Chile, Argentina, Australia, and New Zealand. The beauty of skiing in those countries is that they have winter when we have summer.

One final thought concerning ski trips: take all snow reports, good or bad, with a grain of salt. Generally speaking, snow conditions are most stable and reliable in the West, but you must realize that snow conditions change constantly. Good skiing can turn into something a lot worse than that overnight and vice versa. Unless there is a complete washout, assume that there will be some worthwhile skiing. Your chances are better than 50-50 that you will have a good time despite dire forecasts. Be an all-weather skier. It makes skiing a lot more exciting.

7

SKIING FUN THE EASY WAY: TOURING

I have mentioned touring several times in the course of this book as an easy and inexpensive way to go skiing. What is it? What's involved in equipment and technique? How much does it really cost? Is it for your family?

On the several occasions when I've put the answers on paper, the technical aspects of touring were so simple, they almost weren't worth explaining. But on reflection, this very simplicity may be why it has been ignored by the American public. In the vernacular, it doesn't have pizzazz.

At the same time, some confusion exists between the Alpine and the Nordic versions of skiing. This would explain why more enthusiastic campers, hikers, and walkers have not taken up ski touring. They don't understand that it isn't the same thing as the more common and expensive Alpine sport.

Touring is a rather loosely used word. Any form of skiing without lifts is called touring, but actually a distinction should be made between the Scandinavian version, which is done over relatively gentle, rolling terrain, and the Alpine version, which is done on mountains very similar to those on which our ski areas are located. Most purists refer to the Scandinavian version as touring, the Alpine version as ski mountaineering.

Although the dividing line between the two versions grows a little thin at times, there can be no mistake about what moti-

A version of skiing which is more congenial to family fun—hiking on snow, really—is Scandinavian touring, which is done on easy, rolling terrain on light-weight skis.

vates the touring skier in contrast with the downhill-only skier. The touring skier seeks the benefits of the outdoors during winter and skis are the means to this end. The downhill-only skier is primarily motivated by the thrill of speed and the challenge of the terrain that confronts him. One motivation is no less worthy than the other, but unfortunately our way of life discriminates against touring. It deserves a better fate.

If you have a pair of skis, you can tour. Scandinavian touring uses special equipment, but if your tours are modest ones, this is not essential. With a few modifications your Alpine equipment will work quite well, although the reverse cannot be said about the use of Scandinavian touring equipment in Alpine conditions.

For the majority of skiing families the best approach probably is to buy Alpine equipment rigged in such a way that it can be adapted to touring. This requires little more than a binding which will clamp your toe to the ski while leaving your heel free to move up and down as you are walking and gliding along. A cable binding with a touring attachment that prevents the release toe unit from pivoting will do the job. For walking along the flat or climbing, simply unhitch the cable from the rear cable guides so that your heel is free to move. A pair of "skins" which can be fastened to the bottoms of the skis and prevent backslip on long uphill climbs and a variety of waxes to cope with various snow conditions complete your outfit.

This slightly oversimplifies the requirements. For instance, the less rugged members of your family will find that regular Alpine ski boots are much too stiff, particularly in the sole, and that the polyethylene bottoms of most Alpine skis do not hold wax well. They will also discover that their skis are on the

Not all skiing requires lifts. If you are willing to provide your own uphill power, a whole new world of ski adventures await you and your family. Skiing unaided by lifts in the high mountains is called ski mountaineerng.

heavy side after a mile or so. And that their poles are on the short side for putting drive and push into their gliding walk.

If your touring ambitions are modest, you will put up with these inconveniences but if you feel that touring is your real cup of tea, you will want to buy real Scandinavian touring equipment.

Unlike your Alpine outfit, which may run to $200 or more, even the best touring equipment available will not run much over $50 for everything—boots, bindings, skis, and poles. Again compared with your Alpine equipment, it will be as light as a feather. As you cover the miles, you will hardly feel the skis on your feet, and if you have good technique you can cover a given distance with less effort than by walking.

The Scandinavians, for whom touring is *the* national sport, have developed the manufacture of touring equipment into a fine art. They build equipment for every level of touring.

There are four basic varieties of touring skis: the extremely lightweight, fragile cross-country racing ski, which is probably the one most familiar to you, but which is unsuitable for anything but skiing in a well-prepared track; the light touring ski, for covering very easy, rolling terrain rapidly; the general touring ski, for use in possibly rough, semimountainous or hilly country; and the mountain touring ski, which comes close to regular Alpine skis, and which can be used, as its name implies, in mountainous areas.

Touring skis are made of wood and most have bare wood bottoms. With the exception of the mountain touring ski, touring skis have no edges, although the corners of the better skis are reinforced with a hard, compressed wood. Wood is used not only because it is low in cost and light in weight, but also because it has the ability to hold wax well. Steel edges are not used because steel does not glide well on snow, and in touring, where there is little help from gravity, the glide is everything.

Naturally, touring boots are built with walking and gliding in mind. The sole is shaped in such a way that it bends easily under the ball of the foot. Since turning—at least sharp turning at high speed—is a minor factor in touring, the boots need

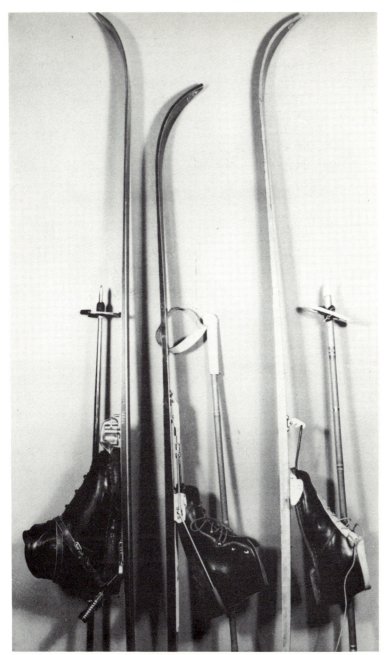

On the left is the equipment you will encounter in the store: Alpine equipment suitably rugged for high speed over difficult terrain. In the center is a touring ski, boot, and pole designed for the more demanding type of Scandinavian touring. At the right is a lighter-weight touring outfit suitable for easy terrain. Note that in the touring skis the heels of the boots are not held fast on the skis. The heel is free to move for easier walking.

give only minimal support. Hence they can be of lightweight construction, using just enough leather to provide a snug, friction-free fit. The ultimate in these boots are the cross-country racing boots, which are little more than glorified track shoes. Most touring skiers find a slightly heavier version with ankle-high uppers more satisfactory.

There are a number of different binding designs. None of them use the release principle because it is neither practical nor necessary. There is enough freedom of movement to prevent injury and it would take an extraordinary accident to produce much more than a bruise. The type most suitable for the type of touring you're most likely to do is made along lines somewhat similar to our Alpine cable bindings.

Poles for use in touring are two to three inches longer than those used for Alpine skiing, and the Scandinavians prefer that they be of bamboo or tonkin cane rather than metal since these provide a certain amount of whip, which helps to propel the skier forward as he takes a stride. Except in long, fast tours, however, this is not a critical factor.

The key to a tourer's outfit is his wax kit and it should have waxes to cope with a large variety of conditions. Also needed is a special waxing iron which is heated with a fuel tablet for melting on the running wax and a cork to rub the wax down to the right smoothness. These items are sometimes hard to find even in specialty stores. Keep a good supply on hand so that you won't run out.

Cross-country waxes and "klisters" (soft-snow waxes that are as sticky as they sound) are specially formulated to prevent backslip when walking on the level or uphill. Contradictory as it may seem, the wax that glides the best will also do the best job of preventing backslip. This is seldom accomplished by only one type of wax. Usually it takes a mixture or separate layers of two or more waxes to get the ideal combination for a given snow condition. Conditions varying between cold, fresh snow and soft warm snow are particularly difficult to wax for.

It is possible to get incredibly involved in waxing, and there is a great deal of mumbo jumbo about it in touring and cross-country circles. The important thing, however, is to learn to recognize the various snow conditions and check the thermometer. The instructions on the various tubes and cans of waxes and klisters are quite specific, and if you follow recommendations, you're not going to be far off. If, once you are under way, the skis pick up snow, it means that you haven't conditioned the skis to snow temperature or you used too warm or soft a wax. If your skis backslip, you either did not apply the wax heavily enough, polished it down too smoothly, or you waxed too cold or hard. You can correct the situation by applying a coat of the appropriate wax over the existing coat, rewaxing from time to time as the wax wears off. If you've followed instructions—most wax companies put out waxing manuals—you'll never be so far off that you have to rewax completely.

Probably the simplest part of touring is the technique, and it doesn't require much instruction to master the fundamentals. The basic touring stride is essentially a swinging type of hiking stride with a slight pause between each stride to allow the skis

Touring is for the family.

to glide. The more efficient the stride the longer the glide, and
the less effort involved. The efficiency of the stride depends on
good coordination between the "kick" (the pushing off from
one ski) and the thrust of the pole with the opposite arm, and,
of course, the wax. This basic "diagonal" stride can be varied
to avoid monotony by double poling (planting both poles while
kicking), and other, more subtle refinements. The top cross-
country racers can travel about 15 miles an hour over sharply
rolling country by using these basic techniques. A reasonably
competent tourer should have no difficulty in traveling at
speeds of over five miles an hour for a prolonged period of
time.

The key to the transition from merely slogging along on
touring skis to touring pleasure is the development of an un-
hurried, smooth, rhythmic stride. It does more for the tourer
than sheer physical stamina. No matter how strong you are,

The basic touring stride is an easy lope. By letting the skis slide between steps,
ground can be covered at jogging speeds with relatively little effort.

if your movements are jerky and uncoordinated, you will tire quickly even on easy terrain.

Because touring speeds are slow (in comparison with Alpine skiing speeds) and terrain relatively easy, turns are not particularly difficult. The tourer steps around the turn in a series of small steps, moving one ski at a time much as a skater will do. If he is in more of a hurry, a simple stem turn with most of the weight on the back of the skis will get him around. A skier trained in Alpine skiing is going to find this tricky because instinctively he will lean forward as he goes into his turn. This will not work with a free heel. If the skier leans forward in a touring turn, he will simply fall on his face.

Except for a crude stem turn, most of the Alpine turns will not work with touring skis. Most turns are made as demonstrated above—by stepping around.

The skier who comes to touring without Alpine experience will not have this difficulty since he will do what comes naturally when faced with a turn—sit back.

Although touring and Alpine technique seem somewhat contradictory in approach, few skiers experience real difficulty in going from one technique to the other or in switching back and forth. Touring is a more adventurous way to get started since it allows the skier a greater range of skiing experiences after a minimum of instruction. Alpine skiing is a somewhat more difficult discipline and a less interesting experience until at the very least a snowplow turn is mastered, but it does give the skier the advantage of greater confidence in difficult terrain and snow conditions. However, both approaches to skiing are useful insofar as they teach mobility on skis. This mobility is fundamentally more important to the beginning skier than any specific maneuver he may learn.

In the Scandinavian countries, touring is the national winter sport. There are thousands of miles of maintained touring trails both in and out of the cities. For lunch, families bring along a picnic and settle down by the side of the trail, just as though it were summer. Even the family dog comes along. This economical form of skiing is gaining popularity in the United States.

If one type of sport has any real advantage over the other, it is that touring can be done on a shoestring, except for the initial investment in equipment. Occasionally you will have to repair or replace equipment, periodically you will have to get a fresh supply of wax and some new heating tablets for your waxing iron, but beyond that there are few additional expenses of any significance. Except for the fact that your tours will be relatively limited in scope until your children are about nine or ten, touring is an ideal family winter outdoor recreation.

Where can you tour?

Almost anywhere where there is snow. One of the charms of touring is that you can haul the skis out any time there is snow, which can be as little as three inches in your local park.

Of course, if you make real trips through the woods and over the hills, the experience will be a great deal more interesting. After selecting a locality for your touring adventure, get a detailed topographic map (1:25,000), published by the U.S. Geodetic Survey, showing hiking trails and logging roads. The latter are especially good for light to moderate touring since they frequently have some sort of shelter along the way. These shelters are important if you get a bad break in the weather or if you plan an overnight trip.

Longer trips in unfamiliar country require careful planning for unexpected contingencies—bad weather, unmapped obstacles, detours, exhaustion of a member of your party, injury—so that there is always a margin of safety. Since tourers travel lightly clothed compared with Alpine skiers, each member of the party should carry with him in a rucksack a parka, a sweater, a pair of so-called warm-up pants or sweat pants, and a spare pair of socks. Somewhere in the party should be a waxing kit, tools for making minor repairs and adjustments, and a spare tip, which can be screwed on the ski in case of breakage.

It is not a good idea to camp overnight in the open. A good tent and sleeping bags will provide adequate shelter, but unless you are really and truly hardy outdoor types, the chances are you will find it difficult to get comfortable. Overnight stops should be made where creature comforts are available. Furthermore, carrying all that equipment and food can make traveling difficult, particularly if you have to carry the younger members' share.

This, of course, raises the question of your child's participation in touring. How long and how demanding should the tour be?

Obviously, the answer will depend on the child and the nature of the terrain available. If your youngster has no trouble covering five miles on a summer Boy Scout hike, he should have no difficulty covering the same distance on touring skis, particularly after he has mastered the art of ski touring. His endurance will also depend on the interest of the tour. If the tour includes opportunities to observe animals or to follow tracks, he will be stimulated to extend himself more than if the tour is devoid of these attractions.

In trying to make judgments about your children's capabilities, a good rule of thumb is that they usually can do in winter what they can do in summer—with one important limitation: in the winter it is not always possible to rest at the point where the youngster runs out of steam. You should schedule your rest stops carefully, preferably where there is shelter. And you should always insist that he dress warmly whenever there is an extended stop. Beyond these precautions, ski touring is much like summer hiking.

If your family enjoys touring, the chances are good it will also enjoy ski mountaineering. The glories of this sport have been widely celebrated because it combines many of the leisurely charms of touring with the down-mountain thrills of Alpine skiing.

Is it for you and your family?

Perhaps, but even then with caution and only in the company of experienced ski mountaineers who know their way around in avalanche country. Before you try it, you should be a good Alpine skier and have some experience with deep-snow skiing. Otherwise, the experience will be anything but happy.

Does this put ski mountaineering out of your reach?

If you really love the outdoors in winter, it is a good bet that you will be a good skier. And you will be a good skier because those mountains you want to ski are there.

8

THE COMPETITION QUESTION

When there are young skiers in the family, it is almost inevitable that you will have to weigh the problem of whether you should let your child race or not. Fortunately, the structure of ski competition makes it possible to resolve the issue in easy stages. With a knowledge of fundamentals, you should have no difficulty in coming to a decision.

In skiing, there are two basic forms of competition: Nordic and Alpine. Nordic competition involves either jumping or cross-country or a combination of the two called Nordic combined. Alpine competition means down-mountain racing in three events—downhill, slalom, and giant slalom.

Nordic competition in the United States has only a limited following and programs for training a youngster in jumping and cross-country are hard to find. Obviously, cross-country is the safest of the ski competitions, but it puts a special premium on physical condition and health. Simple as cross-country may be on a recreational level, on a competitive basis it is a complex endeavor calling for greater athletic skill than is generally realized. Precision technique is essential, something that becomes more readily understandable when you realize that if you slip back only one inch at every stride, a one-mile race will be lost by 70 feet. In addition, stamina is essential. Most top competitors do not develop this kind of stamina until they are in their twenties.

121

Alpine racing has three events: downhill, slalom, and giant slalom.

Although jumping seems like the ultimate in daring, it is not as dangerous as most people think. True, courage is an important factor, but the consequences of a fall are rarely serious, even on a big jump. A jumping hill is designed in such a way that a falling jumper has roughly the same trajectory as the outrun (the landing area). Combined with the loose bindings jumpers wear, the risk is minimal with proper hill preparation and supervision.

While in this country women's participation in cross-country is still limited (there is no women's jumping), Alpine racing is both a men's and a women's sport. The two sexes don't com-

In ski competition, jumping is done only by men.

pete against each other because men's courses are longer and more difficult, but, in terms of honors to be won, both are equal. For each men's title, there is an equivalent women's title, except in college competition, which is all male.

Cross-country (and alpine) racing is both a men's and women's sport. The two sexes don't compete against each other, but there are equivalent titles for each.

The downhill is the premier event of Alpine skiing. As its name implies it is a race down the mountain and there are only enough gates to keep the racer away from dangerous obstacles and to keep his speed within the limits of safety. Gates in all Alpine races consist of two poles with a flag on top of each. The gates are widest in downhill, narrowest in slalom. The racer must pass both feet between the two poles in order to make a legal passage through the gate. Straddling a pole, that is passing with one ski on the outside of the pole, or missing the gate completely results in disqualification. For this reason, each gate is watched by a gatekeeper.

In contrast to downhill, the gates in slalom are not only narrower, but much closer together. To the inexperienced observer, a slalom course is a veritable jungle of gates, but a

A junior skier waits in the starting gate for the signal to start his run in the downhill.

Junior racer rounds gate during practice run.

skilled racer will pass through this jungle faster than most people ski the same distance without gates. A downhill course is set to test the racer's ability to cope with all kinds of terrain variations at high speed, but a slalom is primarily a test of the racer's turning skill and ability to analyze a skiing problem. By setting the gates in various combinations, the course setter can develop a test for every level of competition. (Simple slaloms are frequently used by ski schools to teach precision in turning.)

Giant slalom is a compromise between downhill and slalom and most nearly represents the type of skiing done by the recreational skier. There are no long straight stretches (schusses) as in downhill, but the gates are wider and farther apart than in slalom. Giant slalom courses are always longer than slalom courses, but have approximately the same number of gates (about 60). In major men's competition, there are two runs of giant slalom in a race, just as in slalom. The racer who has the fastest combined time is the winner.

There is competition in both Alpine and Nordic events for every age bracket and every level of skill, from the youngest to the oldest, from the duffer to the super-expert. If there is interest in competition in your family, there is no lack of opportunities to exercise it.

On the informal level, most ski clubs run some sort of race at least once a season, usually an easy giant slalom. Many ski areas also have weekly standard races in which the racers ski down a permanent course and must beat a certain pre-established time in order to win a gold, silver, or bronze medal. Some of these standard races, such as Sun Valley's Golden Sun, are highly regarded. Many areas also stage special children's races involving lots of fun and games.

Any of these informal races may be the place to give your child a taste of competition. Participation in one or two races, even if they are informal, will give you a fairly good clue as to

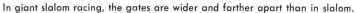

In giant slalom racing, the gates are wider and farther apart than in slalom.

Downhill racing is not for the youngster who is ill grounded in fundamentals or ill equipped technically.

whether his interest is genuine or just the result of a momentary bit of excitement.

While it is generally best to let the decision to race to be the child's own, a little bit of gentle encouragement will not do any harm. Quite frequently the urge is there, but the will to say so isn't. A question to that effect is usually all it takes to determine your youngster's desire; taking him to watch a race may have the same effect. But most children will let you know when they get the urge, and you may find yourself having to make a decision whether yours should or shouldn't.

Informal racing is so much a part of the recreational skiing scene, there is no consequence one way or another if you should decide to let your child race. The courses are easy and no more risky than recreational skiing. If your youngster enjoys it, well and good. If he doesn't, he can quit without loss of face. The trick at this stage is to keep a certain equanimity. By all means praise him if he does well and console him if he doesn't, but don't go overboard. He may interpret excessive praise as your way of telling him that he should race. He may also use excessive condolences as an excuse to feel sorry for himself. A calm outlook will help him keep his sense of proportion about competition and in the long run will help him to be a better competitor if his inclinations run that way.

The competition question becomes a little more serious if he wants to participate in formal racing. A good deal more is involved than in informal racing, and you may well want to nip the project in the bud before it gets out of hand.

It should be almost needless to say that your child should be a good skier before he tries anything much more serious than a kiddie or club race. Unfortunately, it cannot be stressed enough. The ranks of junior racers are full of youngsters who are ill equipped technically to cope with the majority of the simplest junior race courses. Which is too bad. Many a promising youngster's competitive career is thwarted by incomplete mastery of the fundamentals.

You should not rely on your own judgment alone to determine if your child is technically equipped to be a racer. More

Racing is hard on equipment and the Alpine racer particularly has special needs. A racing helmet is required by the rules for downhill and, in some cases, for giant slalom as well.

Victory is its own reward and in ski racing extraordinarily difficult to achieve. Youngsters have to recognize that the climb to the top is tough and that it takes time and training to get there.

than surface appearance or even the ability to negotiate a steep slope is involved. The opinion of a race-wise ski instructor or a coach should be solicited and followed. If this opinion is on the negative side (prefaced by yes, but . . . or no, unless . . .) make sure your child understands this. How hard he works to correct his shortcomings will give you a strong clue as to whether the effort that *you* will have to put in his racing is worth it.

First of all, be aware that junior racing is expensive, both in time and in money. To race well, practice is essential. Practice for ski racing requires at least some daily conditioning and at least two days of skiing a week every week there is an opportunity to do so. A normal ski season lasts from three to four months. The bill for this activity alone is going to be substantial unless you are fortunate enough to have a suitable ski area close to home.

While the equpiment needs of a young racer in the lowest two classifications are not particularly complicated, what there is of it should be first class and will cost no less than $150 and more likely closer to $200. Also you will have to replace the equipment every year. As he progresses in racing, he will need special skis for downhill, slalom and giant slalom and a spare pair of boots and poles. His bindings will have to be the very best. He will need special clothing.

As if this were not enough, you will have to resign yourself to acting as chauffeur, driving him to various meets in diverse sections of your ski region. This may involve 300 or more miles three or four times a season at the start, more often as he climbs through the ranks. In addition, you may have the dubious privilege of being tabbed as a race official, which means that your skiing day consists of one cramped run down from the gate you've been frigidly watching.

I have deliberately painted the picture at its blackest because there may be long stretches where it is just that and where your sense of humor and parental pride are the only restraints that keep you from ditching junior and his racing over the nearest cliff. Once you are resigned to the worst, every little bit of help will make you feel better and, surprisingly, there is a remarkable amount of help available if you will look and ask for it.

Ski competition in the United States is the responsibility of the United States Ski Association (USSA). The USSA in turn is a member of the Federation International de Ski (FIS), which is the international governing body of skiing. All competitions should follow FIS rules, and while exceptions can be made to allow for local or regional circumstances, the FIS rules regarding safety must be carefully observed.

The USSA itself sanctions only so-called national meets, which are only a small number of all the sanctioned ski races in the United States. The remainder are sanctioned and supervised by the USSA's eight regional divisions. The regional divisions also have the duty of classifying racers, both according to skill and by age.

In order to become classified, a racer must apply for a classification card. He can apply to his division directly, but usually it is to his advantage to apply through his ski club.

Racers are juniors until they are 18 years old—class IV if they are 11 and under; class III from 12 through 13; class II from 14 to 15; and class I from 16 through 17. Until a racer becomes a veteran at age 27, he is a senior.

A junior skier shows good form in a giant slalom race.

In addition to classification by age, participation in a race is limited to a particular skill class—D being the lowest and A the highest. All juniors III and IV are classified as D's; all juniors I and II from C to A. Racers can participate in any skill class for which they qualify. For instance, a junior A can race in a senior A race.

Racers are promoted from one class to the next based on the points they earn in each race. These so-called FIS points are calculated from a table and are based on the winning time and the amount of time the subsequent finishers were behind the winner, the winner getting zero points for his efforts.

Getting to the top in ski racing isn't simple. Because of the collision hazards involved, racers go down the course one at a time, running against the clock. Since each racer chews up the course a little—a lot if it isn't properly prepared—the early runners have an advantage over late runners, who may have to run in deep ruts. To determine starting position, racers are ranked in groups of 15 according to their FIS points, the best racers going into the group that runs first, the reasoning being that they earned this position through successful racing. This isn't quite fair, but so far no one has been able to come up with a better system. In any event, part of the job of a young racer

When it comes to competition, it's best to be realistic. It can be dangerous, particularly Alpine racing.

is not only to make a do or die dash for victory, but to improve his FIS points so that he is in a position to win or place well consistently.

If you've had any experience with Little League baseball or any other junior sports program, you are aware that parents, as a rule, do not make good coaches. Competition success is largely a matter of mental and physical discipline and very few parents have the detached outlook required to apply it to their own offspring. Make the most of any program that enables you to take the coaching chore off your back.

There are all kinds of programs for junior racing. The Jaycees have developed an interesting short course of six sessions which will initiate a young racer into the finer points of all phases of skiing competition. The Buddy Werner leagues carry this approach a step further with a system of team racing, which has the advantage of taking some of the pressure off the individual youngster. Beyond the age of 14, the top age limit of these programs, the burden is carried by ski clubs and ski areas, which either have an all-encompassing junior program with a racing class for those who excel, or who have special racing teams. At the very least, they will provide coaching and reduced-rate lift tickets. At their best they will also supply free lift passes to all the various helpers, uniforms, and occasionally transportation to the races.

A good racing program can cut the cost of racing for your youngster considerably. However, in return for these favors you are expected to give service in kind. These services involve hill preparation, officiating, driving a group of youngsters to the races, chaperoning, and helping with paper work and other club activities, and, inevitably, fund raising. Some of these chores are onerous, but well worth while if they relieve you of some of the cost of racing and save you some of the time consumed in making sure that your youngster is where he is supposed to be, either for training or racing.

No matter how great the promise of your child as a racer, be at all times prepared to give him an easy way out. Racing is a hazardous sport, and anything but total enthusiasm can in-

If your youngster is interested in racing, make sure he's enrolled in a properly supervised program so that the risks of injury are minimized to the greatest extent possible.

crease the risks to a considerable extent. Of course, you should be able to distinguish between momentary frustration and discouragement from real loss of appetite for the sport, but if the latter is the case don't pressure him to carry on. He may come around again after a while, but if he doesn't, he still has the other pleasures of skiing.

Speed afoot, great endurance, and sound technique are essentials for cross-country racers. Most good competitors don't mature until they're in their middle twenties.

These can last a lifetime. They should be carefully protected.

9

TIPS FOR THE SKIING FAMILY

Lack of accurate information and advice is one of the major problems of the skiing family. Where to ski, where to buy used equipment, where to find special ski programs, where to find the secretary of the ski club?

The best source of information without engaging in a lot of letter writing and long-distance telephoning is the local ski shop. If the shop doesn't have the information you want at its fingertips, it can usually point you in the right direction so that you can get what you want with a minimum of difficulty.

A second good course of information is the local ski club. Among them, the members of the club have a wide variety of experiences with ski areas, equipment, and other problems that concern skiing families. One of them should be able to answer the question that you may have.

The various ski publications—*Skiing* and *Ski* in particular —are also good sources of information. However, you may have to dig through back issues to find the precise bit of information you want.

Transportation is probably the skier's most difficult problem, particularly when the children want to ski on a day when parents can't for one reason or another.

Not one of the least reasons for joining a ski club or attaching yourself to a group interested in skiing is that they make some sort of car pool arrangement possible. Most skiing parents are more than happy to take someone else's children along —it relieves the monotony of longer trips for their own youngsters—providing that you are willing to reciprocate on some other occasion.

While many communities and ski areas have programs for children, there are a good many that don't, or have only specialized programs that don't suit the needs of your youngsters.

Even though you may be only a relative neophyte in skiing, don't be afraid to start your own program or to take steps to develop such a program within your own community.

On the most primitive level, a group of parents can get together and hire the services of a ski instructor (or coach, if racing is involved) and divide the cost among themselves. This used to be quite common a few years ago, but is rarely done now because all kinds of organizations are willing to sponsor children's programs. These organizations are in a better position to tap much-needed know-how and to secure the cooperation of ski areas and ski schools.

Here are some organizations that have sponsored children's programs: newspapers, radio stations, service organizations (such as the Junior Chamber of Commerce, Lions Club, and Rotary Club), local recreation departments, and various athletic organizations.

Schools only rarely have a competitive skiing program and even more rarely a recreational skiing program. The reasons for not including skiing in the physical education program are numerous and varied, and as far as the skier is concerned, probably irrelevant. However, change is a long drawn-out process. Your children may be out of school before your pleas meet with a favorable response. Nevertheless, in recent years, the solid wall of school administration opposition has been cracked and you may have better luck.

There's a tendency these days to stress the maintenance-free character of equipment. For your own safety and skiing enjoyment, it is best not to believe a word of this. It is true that ski equipment needs a lot less maintenance than was the case a few years ago, but it still needs some.

Binding, of course, should be checked periodically for correct setting, and the moving parts should also be treated from time to time with silicon spray, grease or oil as recommended by the manufacturer. These lubricants tend to wash out with use and while the skis are being transported to and from the ski area.

The need for sharp edges on hard snow or ice cannot be overstressed. Even the best edges will grow dull with the result that the skis will not hold when the snow gets hard. An edge sharpener or a file will remedy the problem if you know how to handle these tools. If you are the do-it-yourself type, you can have all sorts of fun. There are numerous ways of treating edges. Your ski shop or your ski instructor can give you more specific instructions.

Boots should not only be cleaned and polished according to the manufacturer's instructions, but several other points need careful watching and fixing as necessary: laces, the binding notches, the buckles (if your boot is of that type), and the state of the seams. Good care of boots can easily add another season of use to their life.

Your ski shop will be more than happy to do these chores for you. However, even if you are not a habitual do-it-yourselfer, try to get a passing acquaintance with these maintenance procedures. Knowing how will not only save you money, but also will greatly increase your skiing enjoyment. It can mean the difference between a bad day and a good day on skis.

If you have to travel considerable distances to ski, give some thought to how you will keep your children amused during the trip. Keep in mind that a ski trip is not quite the same thing as a summer outing, where casual stops don't make much difference. On a ski trip you're trying to get to a specific place at a fairly specific time.

Although station wagons have drawbacks from a handling point of view, they're probably the most suitable vehicles for family ski trips. The wagon can be fixed up so that the children can take naps or play with toys.

There are numerous other ways of keeping children amused, and these are limited only by your imagination. For instance, my particular favorite is to note the historical markers along the way. They are the source of endless stories that will keep children goggle-eyed for an hour at a time.

A double is more or less the standard unit in ski lodges. Children are usually accommodated in rollaway beds at a small additional cost—about $3 to $4.

If you have a larger family or friends good enough to share a weekend or a vacation with, you might weigh the possible economies of renting a condominium apartment. These apartments cost anywhere from $25 to $60 a day, depending on their size and the area in which they are located. If enough people are involved, the per-person, per-day cost can be considerably lower than at a lodge. Additional savings are possible in such an apartment if you do your own cooking. Of course, it is up to you to determine whether you want to spend your vacation or your weekend away from home working in a kitchen.

If you ski regularly at one ski area, investigate the availability of ski lockers. These lockers enable you to store your equipment at the area and, aside from their convenience, save wear and tear on the equipment and protect it against theft when you go in the lodge. The cost of a locker usually is between $15 and $25 a season.

Perhaps one of the most painful stages for a skiing family to go through is that when a child becomes aware of brand names (usually expensive) of equipment and wants to own a particular brand of ski, binding, or boot, even though the advantage to him is only marginal at best.

With some children it is possible to jolly them along until they get over this phase. Unfortunately, skiing, like everything else these days, is immersed in promotional material and most parents find it difficult to turn off the preoccupation with brands.

Old-fashioned though it may be, the most satisfactory way in the long run is to give the youngster the hard facts of life. If he wants a particular item, he will have to earn the money for it by delivering newspapers or mowing lawns. Usually, one exposure to the experience of earning his equipment is sufficient to cure him of his brand consciousness, particularly if he realizes that the benefits are marginal at best.

You can also help the youngster along with some do-it-yourself know-how. It's not difficult to sew racing stripes on pants or to decorate skis and boots so that they look like something even more special in his eyes than the brand model.

Since you'll be anxious to have your family's ski equipment stay in good condition and maintain its value, you will have to make provision for proper storage between ski trips. Any cool, ventilated spot will do. A rack-type arrangement to keep the skis upright and out of any water (commercial units specifically designed for this purpose are available, although it is not difficult to build your own), a few pegs for ski poles, and a shelf for storing boots will do the job.

Skis should be dried off to prevent rusting and corrosion before they are put away. If you live in a section where the roads are salted, you may have to go a step further and wash them off first. Salt is particularly hard on bindings and edges.

When storing skis for the summer, do not store metal and plastic skis under tension. As long as the storage area is reasonably cool, the skis will maintain their proper shape and camber. When storing wood skis, block the skis, but not directly against each other. The best way is to buy a top quality, squared-up piece of 2 by 4 and to strap the skis against that, one ski on each side. Insert a block of wood just thick enough to maintain the normal amount of camber (between a half and three-quarters of an inch).

Boots should be stored in boot trees at all times. The way to keep them dry, both between trips and during storage in summer, is to stuff them with newspapers.

If there are no touring buffs in your local ski club or among the skiers you know, you may find them in one of your local conservation societies or outdoor clubs. If this fails, write to Chairman, Ski Touring Council, U.S. Ski Association, 1726 Champa St., Denver, Colo. 80202. He can refer you to the nearest touring group or enthusiast.

Traveling as a group, either by bus or plane, makes sizable economies in travel costs possible. Charters are usually half of the regular fare.

However, you should be aware of the pitfalls, particularly as far as charters are concerned. Perhaps the biggest drawback is that you have to go and return with the charter group. This means that both the dates and duration of the trip may not suit your particular travel plans and convenience. In addition, there is always the risk that the charter bus or plane will not be filled to capacity, in which case you may have to pay an additional sum to make up the difference between the projected fare based on capacity and the number of passengers that finally go on the charter. Finally, sad to say, some charter operators have been known to evade legal requirements, and you may discover that you have made extensive vacation plans with no way to get there.

While charters are most subject to these pitfalls, any group travel arrangement suffers from these potential weaknesses. Before entering any group travel agreement, make sure that the organizer can deliver what he is promising, and be sure to calculate the cost to you if he doesn't. And, where possible, take out insurance (about $10 per person on a European charter trip) just in case something goes sour.

By shopping wisely, there are several ways to save on clothing and equipment.

The most obvious way to save is to take advantage of the end-of-season sale that is held by every ski shop. Except on fair-traded items, reductions of 20 per cent or more are possible by waiting for these sales, which start anywhere from mid-January on. In addition, many shops have preseason sales to clear out clothing and equipment held over from the previous season.

If you do want to take advantage of sales, you have to recognize that selection may well be limited. So don't count on getting everything that your family needs on sale.

It is also quite possible to become sales happy—to be penny wise and pound foolish. Unless there is a good part of the ski season left, it rarely makes sense to buy children's boots (and almost anything else that has to fit) at an end-of-season sale. By the time the child gets to use the boots, he may already have outgrown them.

In the case of difficult fitting problems, the time to start shoping is as soon as the ski shops and departments open for business. This may not save you money as a sale would, but may avoid a more expensive solution simply because you have the item right away. Even if the item you need is not immediately available, early shopping will enable you to order it in time for the ski season.

Finally, having made an investment in skiing, do your share to promote the sport. Encourage—gently—others to participate. Join a ski club. And support the various local, regional, and national ski programs. There may not be any direct dollars and cents return to you, but there will be long-range benefits— if not for you, then for your children and grandchildren. You will not only help to perpetuate our outdoor heritage, but by skiing you will enrich it.

GLOSSARY OF SKI TERMS

Alpine—Basically anything referring to mountain skiing, but specifically any type of skiing in which the primary objective is to ski down-mountain.

Angulation—A fundamental movement of skiing involving the bending away of the upper body from the slope to compensate for the movement of the knees into the slope. Done to control edges and shift body weight.

Counter-rotation—A movement that involves turning the upper body in a direction opposite to that of the lower body.

Christie (or Christiania)—Any turn in which the skis are parallel during the end phase of the turn.

Edging, edge set—A way of controlling the sideways motion of the skis by increasing or decreasing the amount of edge bite on the snow, usually done by rolling the knees in and out from the hill. An edge set is an emphatic edging motion used to create a platform for starting the turn.

Fall line—the most direct and steepest way down a slope.

Inside ski—The ski on the inside of the turn, or turn to be. Also the parts of the body on the inside of the turn are referred to as inside shoulder, inside arm, etc.

Inside edge—Always the edge on your ski that is parallel to the inside of your foot regardless of whether the ski is the inside or outside ski of the turn.

Geländesprung—Called *geländie* in the American vernacular. A German word meaning terrain jump.

Nordic—Basically anything referring to skiing over easy, rolling terrain without the aid of lifts. In competition, Nordic events include cross-country racing over various distances and jumping.

Outside ski—The ski on the outside of the turn, usually the weighted ski.

Outside edge—Always the edge on the outside of your foot.

Parallel—Any maneuver in which the skis remain parallel to each other. Hence, parallel christie, a turn in which the skis are parallel throughout the turn. It does not necessarily follow that the skis must be close together.

Rotation—A movement of the upper body that involves turning the upper body in the direction of the turn to help initiate the turn. Modern rotational movements are also called anticipation.

Schuss—Loosely used, any form of skiing straight. More accurately, it is skiing straight down the fall line.

Snowplow, snowplow turn—A beginning skiing maneuver in which the skis are spread into a V in order to slow down. In a snowplow the skis are put on their inside edges. A snowplow turn is made by a shift of weight and a manipulation of the edges.

Stem—The basic principle behind a series of turns in which one of the skis is pushed out into a half-V position and then weighted in order to initiate a turn. Hence stem turn, stem christie, etc.

Traverse—Any angle to the fall line; skiing across the fall line.

Unweighting—Reducing the weight on the skis so that the skis can turn. Skis can be unweighted in a number of ways —by hopping, by skiing up on a bump and by brisk up and down motions of the body.

Uphill christie—A turn up or into the hill with the skis parallel; the end phase of most christie-type turns.

Wedeln—A series of short parallel turns.

Weight shift—The shift of body weight from one ski to the other; in stemmed turns the shift of weight to the downhill or outside-ski-to-be during the initiation phase of the turn.